ADVANCE PRAISE

"*Parenting Freedom* is an exploration of the influences that prevent us from being truly present for our lives and the lives of our children. Renee Cachia shares her research and experience to help parents gain insight into their parenting patterns and foster mindfulness to break free of the past. This is a book for parents who are looking to uncover their internal resources and create deeper connections within their families."

—SHARON SALZBERG, AUTHOR OF *REAL HAPPINESS* AND *REAL CHANGE*

"This unmindful world we live in these days doesn't serve us well in many ways, not least of which is that otherwise loving and well-meaning parents can easily get swept up in our collective distraction and stress. Unfortunately, this leads to unconsciously teaching children by example how to also be distracted and stressed. Renee Cachia's insightful book, *Parenting Freedom*, is therefore very much needed and timely. It clearly and insightfully guides parents on a liberating journey all the way from recognizing the problem to arriving at deep and meaningful solutions. If you're a committed parent who wants the best for your children and yourself, read this book."

—ASSOC. PROFESSOR CRAIG HASSED, INTERNATIONALLY RECOGNIZED MINDFULNESS EXPERT AND AUTHOR OF *MINDFULNESS FOR LIFE*

"A must-read for every parent seeking to navigate their inner world and manage stress. Dr. Renee Cachia is an expert in helping parents unlock their limiting self-beliefs and insecurities. A practical handbook to help to lead parents to a place where they can be truly present with themselves and their children."

—MARY HOANG, AUTHOR OF *DARKNESS IS GOLDEN*, PSYCHOLOGIST AND FOUNDER OF THE INDIGO PROJECT

PARENTING FREEDOM

Parenting Freedom

Transform Stress and Depletion to **Connectedness & Meaning**

Dr Renee Cachia

COPYRIGHT © 2021 RENEE CACHIA
All rights reserved.
www.reneecachia.com

PARENTING FREEDOM
Transform Stress and Depletion to Connectedness & Meaning

ISBN   978-1-5445-2156-5 *Hardcover*
       978-1-5445-2155-8 *Paperback*
       978-1-5445-2154-1 *Ebook*

*To all of the people—clients, mentors, and loved ones—
who have opened their hearts and minds to me over the
years. This book is both for you and because of you.*

My love, Jake. This book is yours as much as it is mine.

Contents

AUTHOR'S NOTE 11
INTRODUCTION 13

PART I: STRESS CYCLES
1. SURVIVAL: PROGRAMMED FOR SURVIVAL 23
2. ILLUSIONS: FRAMED FOR FAILURE 37
3. MIND: STORIES ABOUT THE SELF 49
4. UNCONSCIOUS: DEFAULT TO AWARENESS 67

PART II: BREAKING FREE
5. INTERACTION: MINDFUL PARENTING PRACTICE 87
6. TRAITS: CHANGING YOUR BRAIN 105
7. PRESENCE: CULTIVATING MINDFUL STATES 123
8. MEDITATE: A COMMITTED PRACTICE 137

PART III: STAYING FREE
9. COMPASSION: UNLIMITED INTERNAL RESOURCES 155
10. ATTUNEMENT: INSIGHTFUL PARENTING SKILLS 173
11. VALUES: YOUR OWN NAVIGATION SYSTEM 193
12. VISION: LIBERATION AND LIFE POSSIBILITIES 211

ACKNOWLEDGEMENTS 227
ABOUT THE AUTHOR 231
NOTES 233

Author's Note

This book stands on the shoulders of thousands of scientific studies and peer-reviewed journal articles. This body of research takes different psychological approaches, but all articles focus on human potential rather than limitations. As a research psychologist, I have been conditioned to cite all sources possible. However, to make this book more readable, I referenced only the most salient studies in the notes.

The case studies are designed to reflect the experience of many committed and conscientious caregivers, mothers especially. If you can relate to them personally, it is both intentional and a coincidence. I have not included real-life client details to maintain confidentiality.

You are invited to continue the journey on socials @reneecachiaphd and visit my website www.reneecachia.com to access free resources that are designed to support the learnings in this book.

Introduction

Once we become aware of our patterns, we are never the same again. We have the privilege and the freedom of choice.

The complexity of raising a child often involves cyclical stress patterns and subconscious forces that drive our unhelpful habits. Particular reactions that tend to repeat themselves blindside us. This is a natural part of the human experience. We fall victim to our conditioning, which shapes our view of the world and our behaviour more than we realise, if we realise it at all.

Love, fear, and shame are powerful emotions at play when parenting. When paired with chronic stress, they can reinforce unhelpful negative cycles in our minds, which tend to shape our parenting habits and exert effects on our children. The continuity of daily domestic struggles, stress, anxiety, and fear for our child's future—taken together with deep love and a primal need to protect our children—leaves good-willed parents feeling depleted, rarely finding homeostasis of their body, contentment of their mind, or vitality of their spirit.

This is not a book on how to parent. Rather, it is a book *for* committed parents who are burned out. It is written for loving parents who are tired of being tired and victims to their stress cycles, making them doubt their inherent parenting ability. Every conscientious parent I have ever met has the purest intentions: to be the most loving, supportive, and nurturing parent that they can be. They want to use their power to instil good values, moral virtues, and meaning so that their child can be happy, resilient, and walk through life with a healthy level of self-esteem.

Fast forward from conception to childhood, and our pure intentions can fall short. When we face the inevitable adversities that arise at one stage or another, we can lose our confidence and sense of competence as a parent. It's understandable given the landscape of parenting today. Given the alarming mental health statistics, receiving an unexpected diagnosis, and dealing with ongoing behavioural difficulties, paired with never-ending advice from experts and not-so experts, parents are left feeling confused and exhausted. Living in this constant state of hyperarousal reduces our ability to function effectively, physiologically, and psychologically. As a result, even the most well-intended, loving, and compassionate parents can act in ways that are unrecognisable to themselves.

As a psychologist who has worked with thousands of people across generations—children, their parents, and their grandparents—I have had the privilege of observing how our stress cycles and unconscious patterns play out in our everyday lives. As a fellow human, I have experienced my own emotional and psychological struggles and growths that have enabled me to understand these patterns more intimately. While the focus of this book is on how these patterns impact parenting in particular, many of the case studies speak to universal human experiences.

In the earlier days of my career as a young and passionate therapist with a lack of boundaries, I did not have a solid foundation of self-care to sustain my well-being. Although a generally 'resilient' person, I lacked the psychological skills to effectively cope with what I was being exposed to at work: young people with disabilities unable to maintain basic human integrity, running in front of cars, losing their parents, being exposed to domestic violence, and wanting to end their lives or harm themselves.

Without the right support and practices in place, it's not surprising that I landed a pretty severe case of burnout. I lived in a perpetual state of stress and anxiety, had insomnia for the better part of four months, and experienced an unusual amount of weight gain in a short period of time, and full-blown exhaustion. Severely sleep deprived and running off adrenaline and coffee, I pushed through until I was bedridden from lack of sleep.

Through my journey of personal growth and healing, I discovered that my gravitation towards children and adolescents was the result of my own vulnerable inner child, which will make more sense once you have finished this book. We usually develop our deepest passions from our own personal pain points. As the profound Steven Hayes says, 'we hurt where we care, and we care where we hurt'.[1] Well, I care about vulnerable children—a lot. And through the process of developing wisdom from the breadth of my professional experience, I have learnt that this means caring for their parents and their inner children even more.

Once I became aware of my patterns and learnt how to detangle them, I was never the same again. I developed heightened meta-awareness—of attention, myself, and emotions. I now have the ability to recognise early signs of when I start to fall back into old patterns. Putting the brakes on brings conscious choice, which to me, is freedom.

Awareness is the cornerstone to developing insight into the traps and illusions of the mind, the automaticity of the nervous system, the development of neural networks that maintain living in autopilot, as well as the forces of societal, familial, and cultural conditioning that have led us to this unsustainable point in parenting. Operating from our conditioned automaticity, including the inherited beliefs that we have adopted on an intergenerational level, takes away the ultimate privilege of the freedom of choice.

Without conscious awareness, we have no true freedom. We react from stressor to stressor, from one tightly held belief to another, and spend most of our time as slaves to a defensive and often unhelpful aspect of the unconscious mind. This unconscious part of the mind is known in the mainstream as the ego, which primarily works to keep us small and safe, playing a pivotal role in reinforcing unconscious parenting patterns.

This book has been broken down into three parts. In Part 1, we will explore four main factors that perpetuate stress cycles: our stress-dominant state, the illusions of perfection, the stories we tell ourselves, and unconscious default modes. The automatic stress cycles create a barrier between an authentic parent–child connection and unconsciously limit our child's potential despite our good intentions. At the same time, such cycles impact the default mode network in our brain, which ultimately reduces our freedom to choose how to respond, live our lives, and parent our children. At the end of Part 1, it will be clear why we must break these cycles and how we can start increasing our awareness.

Part 2 symbolises the breaking free of our stress cycles and default modes. This includes understanding how we can make imminent, short-term and long-term changes in our state, our brain, and our parenting. We will draw upon the research of neuroscience and neuroplasticity to explore how we can develop new personal traits to enhance our inherent natural parenting skills.

Part 3 will build upon these insights, exploring the most essential factors in staying free. This includes building unlimited internal resources that are more important than self-esteem and empathy. We will also explore how these compassionate resources can help us become more consistent when parenting and setting loving limits for our children.

These new resources will help us embody the most important parenting skill there is: emotional attunement. It does not matter which way we look at the research—from attachment theory, emotion-focussed, or even behavioural perspective—it all comes down to our responsiveness to the child who is in front of us. The more mindful and present we are with our children, the more attuned we naturally become to ourselves and to our children. This promotes responsiveness to our child's personality, temperament, and unspoken needs. In turn, we become more aware of and responsive to our needs by developing an internal navigation system. We explore some practical and relatable case studies that show how we can reflect on our values to make important, but often resisted, changes when parenting.

The intention of this book is to help you navigate a calmer, more conscious, and empowered parenting life. You will learn how to develop new psychological skills to create lasting and meaningful change to stay connected—to yourself, to your children, and to the world around you. Together, these changes will shift the tone of your family and your life. I've touched on my personal journey to finding freedom, and now, I carve the path for you.

PART I

Stress Cycles

CHAPTER 1

Survival: Programmed for Survival

On a Thursday evening, Sarah crouches on the floor of the shower with the door locked. Through the speaker of her smartphone, an audiobook plays on how to be a better parent. The perfect parent. 'Children are a reflection of their parents,' the voice says. 'It's your job to prioritise their emotional, social, psychological, and physical well-being... If you don't teach them these things...who else will?'

But Sarah stopped listening minutes ago. Instead, she's crying. She simply cannot compete with the ideal parent that she and society have crafted as her benchmark. Her husband works long hours and travels for work, resulting in high-care demands and daily responsibilities that fall primarily on Sarah, who also works close to full time. Her twelve-year-old son and nine-year-old daughter, like many siblings, are completely different children, challenging Sarah to adapt to each of their needs. This leaves her feeling as though she is constantly failing one, if not the other.

She pauses the audiobook recording mid-sentence and climbs into bed. It's the end of another demanding day. She scrolls through her phone for some 'me time'. She is well aware that being on her phone makes her feel worse, but it's a welcome distraction from her train of repetitive, often unhelpful, thought patterns. She can keep these thoughts at bay during the day, when she's busy. But, as soon as her head hits the pillow, they all start to catch up with her—a sense of dissatisfaction, discontent, and dread for tomorrow.

'Is this *it*? Is being a mother my life purpose?' Next, comes guilt and shame. 'What kind of mother are you? Why can't you just feel grateful like everyone else? Why can't you be more like Claire at drop-off who has all her shit together, and actually seems to like her kids?' Sarah does whatever she can to avoid her deep-seated shame. She reasons with her emotions, tries to talk herself out of these feelings, and ends up mindlessly scrolling recent articles on her phone in an attempt to distract herself. Eventually, she falls asleep.

The alarm goes off at 6:00 a.m., startling her to wake up for another mundane day. After six hours of low-quality sleep, she's still depleted. The accumulation of physiological stress has altered her body's natural clock—her circadian rhythm. This circadian rhythm balances our physiology to adapt to a proper routine. It is what is responsible for keeping us awake to light during the day and making us sleepy in the evening by releasing sleep hormones like melatonin. This twenty-four-hour clock allows us to enter deep sleep cycles and then naturally arise in the morning feeling rested. When we are not in flow with our circadian rhythm, we wake up vulnerable to low moods, negative emotions, and a generally irritable state.

Sarah does not remember what it feels like to wake up feeling refreshed. She has just accepted that having children means saying goodbye to proper sleep. Her body is in a state of constant survival mode. She does not have the resources to shift from the stress response into a state of recovery and rest. When combating stress day in and day out becomes familiar, we start to believe that it is normal. We start to look for other explanations for our associated symptoms. We believe that there must be something wrong with us—with our brain or our body. If we have the tendency to ruminate—replaying situations and memories of the past in our mind—we will most likely come to the same negative conclusion. We are the problem.

Sarah drags herself to the kitchen. She puts water in the

kettle as she heads towards the bedroom wing to wake the kids for school. As she gently opens her son's bedroom door, he makes a grunt, turns his head away, and pulls the covers over his head. Sarah takes his gesture as a sign of disrespect, and her mind starts feeding her memories of all the times that he has disrespected her. He is the child who triggers her the most, though she doesn't know why or have much awareness of the cycle at play.

As Sarah's resentment grows, her heartbeat begins to race, her stomach feels like it's in knots, and her breathing becomes shallow and rapid. Five minutes later, she comes back and sees that he is still in bed. She screams at him to get up. He screams back and demands that she leaves him alone. She screams louder and slams the door. Feeling angry and guilty at the same time, she blames her husband for not being present. Then she blames her son for being difficult. She concludes he is difficult because of her own mum-failure.

She finds her daughter sitting at the kitchen bench quietly eating breakfast. Sarah thanks her for getting herself up and making breakfast. Her daughter's lips curl up in a small, nervous smile.

Sarah marches back down the hallway to ensure that her son starts getting ready for school this time.

'Get up!' she shouts, and then snatches his phone before

she pulls the covers off. Her son screams back, arguing that he hates school and isn't going. She threatens with desperation, 'Get up for school *now* or you lose your phone for the rest of the day.' He doesn't flinch, so she reasserts, 'This is your last chance. Get dressed for school or I will take your devices away for the rest of the week!' Another cycle begins—the power struggle. Finally startled by the sternness in her voice, he reluctantly gets out of bed and starts to get dressed.

At this point, Sarah notices that her heart is racing. Her headache intensifies, and she craves her morning coffee. With little time for her own grooming, nor any time to make a coffee, Sarah gets herself ready as quickly as possible. When everyone is finally ready to go, there is another routine fight to get in the car; her son refuses, she threatens, he eventually gets in. Her daughter rolls her eyes at him, seemingly withdrawn from the ordeal.

When the rocket finally launches, and the kids get out of the car to walk onto the school grounds, Sarah feels sick from the cocktail of stress hormones, her gut feeling of guilt, and her hunger and dehydration.

THE PHYSIOLOGICAL WAR ZONE

Sarah sits in traffic on her way out of the school grounds, feeling bitter towards herself and the world. She thinks about how much she loves her children. She can feel the love deep in her chest. Yet, she wonders why she struggles to show them this unconditional love. Why do they fall into such predictable ordeals every morning? When they get older, would they remember her as the screaming parent who lost control every morning? She wonders if it's possible to love them and not like them at the same time. Would they be better off without her? These self-critical thoughts become louder as she drives, her mood becoming lower and lower.

Sarah is unable to see that she already *is* everything that her children need and more. She's a wonderful mother who, from a primal perspective, is trapped in a cycle of cognitive, emotional, and physiological reactivity that surpasses her good intentions. She internalises such a common scenario as evidence that she is a bad mum, who somehow lacks something.

As she heads to work, she turns up the music to distract her from her anxious thoughts. Her already shallow breathing quickens and her heart races faster as she begins to panic. She questions if she is having a heart attack, ponders if it would be a bad thing, and then scolds herself for having that thought. It's not even nine o'clock in the morning, and she is experiencing full-blown, full-body exhaustion. With a heavy head, she rushes to the local cafe to pick up a croissant and large, extra-strong coffee to-go with a teaspoon of sugar. With a little burst in her blood-sugar levels and energy from the caffeine, her heart races again. Her adrenal glands are alerted to continue to accelerate the production of stress-related hormones, including cortisol, adrenaline, and norepinephrine. Her body recognises this primal stress response and prepares for imminent survival needs. It automatically shuts down unnecessary systems, like the immune system, digestive system, and reproductive system to preserve all energy sources.

This heightened preparedness to stay alive dominates Sarah's mind, body, and spirit and remains present as she commences her workday. But from an outsider's perspective, no one notices the ebbs and flows of her emotions, mood, and energy. She is a master at masking how she is *really* feeling. Her boss views her as bright and high functioning—meeting the demands of her role as an account manager, completing work on time, and maintaining client relationships. As she is a polite, friendly, and well-spoken colleague, most people like her too. Sarah's job provides her with momentary relief from her internal suffering. Unlike at home, she receives positive feedback for her labour. Her feelings of success and distraction from her self-criticism reinforce her preference for her work over her children. This only exacerbates her guilt. She revels in dread as she imagines going home to her physiological war zone, her stress response reactivates, and the cycle repeats.

At lunchtime, Sarah forces a smile when her child-free colleague exclaims that she hopes that one day, she too can balance a career and a family, just like Sarah does. For a second, Sarah wishes they could trade lives, then wishes she could take back her automatic thought. What kind of person would think such a thing? She assumes even a good psychologist wouldn't be able to deal with her. Maybe they would confirm what she already believes about herself deep down.

In a search for answers, Sarah books a ticket to a working parent seminar a week later. When the charismatic speaker is asked how she juggles both business and motherhood, she responds, 'With wine.' The audience laughs, normalising the everyday struggle and the tendency to fall short of finding genuinely helpful tools. They all relate to an overreliance on short-term and sometimes unhelpful escape mechanisms. As the speaker continues to glamourise the struggle, Sarah assumes the other mums must be more competent. More confirmation: there's definitely something wrong with her.

Sarah, like many busy women, has little awareness of the impact her chronic stress response has on the overall quality of her life, both in the short and long term. This is because we don't just normalise but celebrate burnout, in all of its perceived glory. Through external validation, Sarah is socially accepted and praised for being busy and productive. At least she is achieving something, perpetuating the subconscious cycle of stress.

Instead of working *with* her physiology, Sarah unintentionally works *against* it. She perceives her struggles to be a personal fault, a lack of resilience related to her inability to adapt, or a shortcoming of her body as a result of getting older. This is not merely the story of Sarah; it's the story of millions of busy, modern adults. I observe it over and over again with clients who can't seem to break the cycle.

THE AUTONOMIC NERVOUS SYSTEM ON OVERDRIVE

The old-school Western approach to stress management is often focussed on imminent and short-term relief from the discomfort of chronic stress. This is where Eastern understandings of replenishing after burnout of the autonomic nervous system has come to light in recent years, in society and in modern psychology. To break and transform stress cycles in the long term, we must first understand them, be aware of what maintains them, and be open-minded to finding a new way forwards, even if we don't know exactly what that looks like yet.

The stress response is governed by the autonomic nervous system, which is composed of the sympathetic and parasympathetic nervous systems. When the amygdala, an almond-shaped structure located in the limbic system in the brain, detects a distress signal, it communicates with the hypothalamus to activate the sympathetic nervous system. This is commonly referred to as the fight-flight-freeze stress response. From an evolutionary perspective, the amygdala was an asset to our hunting-and-gathering lifestyle. This signal ensured our survival.

Nowadays, due to the repetition and regular occurrence of stressors, the amygdala expands in size and dominance, exerts control over our physiological response, and overrides slower, more rational parts of our brain. This process was coined as the 'amygdala hijack' by psychologist and journalist, Daniel Goleman.[2] The hijack triggers an auto release of stress hormones through the pituitary gland. At the same time, our respiration, heart rate, and blood pressure all increase. As any internal resources that are nonessential to imminent survival shut down, digestion slows, and the immune and reproductive systems are suppressed.

Once the perceived threat passes, the parasympathetic nervous system is designed to correct and counteract some of the damaging effects that the body reactively secretes. Known as the 'rest and digest' system, it is required to restore and replenish the body back to a calmer, more sustainable homeostatic state. We might calm down, but the stress does not just disappear. There are residues of stress that remain: hormonal imbalances, a hypervigilant amygdala, and subconscious impressions that we suppress. Our fear-based nervous system communicates with brain regions that directly impact our mood and motivation. Symptoms of stress, anxiety, and depression are rarely mutually exclusive.

When the amygdala hijacks the brain, our default mode is activated. When we are in default mode, we cannot choose how to respond. This is why we often say we're not going to overreact when our child does not listen, but the next time they ignore us, we launch into fight mode. In fight mode, our unconscious physiological intention is to win. So, we wield power over our child. We ask firmly but with authority, then we yell, and then, we threaten. We may even throw in some insults. It might go something like this: 'Go do your homework now...get off the couch and do your homework now...I don't understand why you have to be difficult all the time.' All parents go into fight mode sometimes. The problem is when it becomes our habitual way of parenting.

Fight mode is about control. The intention is to dominate the interaction with the child. Control rarely leads to connection. In fact, it destroys connection. Such dynamics actually worsen parental stress, because our physiological state becomes determined by our expectations. Unless our child demonstrates a desired behaviour, we struggle to calm down. When parents seek help for behaviour management, they tend to be stuck in this cycle. And so, they see a psychologist for a single consultation or read a blog post, but it doesn't help. Their child is still not listening. The cycle continues. We unconsciously believe that if we learn strategies to win the fight, the problems will go away. Then when they don't, we may go into the freeze response by shutting down, withdrawing, blaming ourselves, and going into shame spirals that cause us to disconnect from our emotions and our child.

For Sarah, she assumed that if she could just get her son out of bed and to school without a fight, then all the other problems would dissipate. But what about her depleted nervous system? What about the state of *her* body and mind? Would the exhaustion just go away? It's quite likely that she would just notice new triggers that activate her stress response. The power struggle would play out in a different way. That's the nature of a cycle. Until we address the larger forces at play, it repeats.

The first step is to start to recognise the stress response in our bodies and notice when we are living in survival mode. As we shift into a more sustainable way of being, it becomes easier to recognise the old traps of survival mode when they inevitably return. Chronic stress does not just disappear the moment we feel imminent relief. Working with our nervous system instead of against it is an ongoing practice. It requires shifts in our lifestyle. These shifts are much easier and much smaller than we perceive. Someone living in a busy city might believe moving to the countryside is the only way to start repairing their nervous system. While this may help, it's the small but regular practices—like meditation and breathwork—that expand our window of tolerance in the nervous system.

Coined by psychiatrist Dan Siegel, the window of tolerance refers to the threshold where we can adaptively respond to stressors in our environment.[3] We all have the internal resources to respond to stressors effectively. When we stay within this window, we are, according to Siegel, in the 'river of well-being'. Our sympathetic nervous system can still be activated. However, we have the resources to activate our parasympathetic nervous system to help us recover. This means we can functionally adapt to the stressors in our environment, to self-regulate our emotions, and to stay mentally present with the ability to take perspectives and respond with flexibility.

TABLE 1. SIEGEL'S WINDOW OF TOLERANCE

HYPERAROUSAL (FIGHT-FLIGHT)	WINDOW OF TOLERANCE	HYPOAROUSAL (FREEZE)
Features: high anxiety, stress, anger, overwhelm, chaos, fight-flight, hypervigilance, outbursts, rigidity	Features: able to respond flexibly, adapt to environment, self-regulate triggers, stay present, prosocial	Features: shut down, numb, withdraw, low mood, shame, guilt, passive, tuned out, autopilot, disconnected

When we fly into fight-flight automatically, our body is dominated by the hypervigilant amygdala. Our responses are usually reactive, rigid, and even chaotic. When adults have a full-blown outburst by a seemingly small trigger, it usually means that they have been simmering on the edge of their window of tolerance for some time, ready to be pushed into a state of hyperarousal. For example, our child begs for chocolate at the supermarket, and our heightened response is disproportionate to their nagging. On the other hand, we can also move into a state of hypoarousal, where we freeze and shut down. This may look like going down a shame spiral, having a low mood, tuning out, disconnecting from emotions, being passive, numbing guilt and so on. For some, this often follows after an extended period of hyperarousal. For example, after our outburst in the supermarket that carries on until we get to the car, we resort to harsh consequences and threats to take away privileges. We then find ourselves in a shame spiral of negative self-talk and struggling with feelings of guilt and failure as a parent, knowing that we overreacted.

To learn how to work with our nervous system, it's important that we start to notice our triggers and the main signs that push us outside our window of tolerance. This will reflect a foundational basis of self-awareness, as we'll learn as we continue reading.

CHAPTER 2

Illusions: Framed for Failure

Kate desperately wants to be a good mother. When she was growing up, she was a competitive runner. She had learned to be disciplined and believed in the importance of self-talk. Positive or negative, this inner monologue kept her in line. Letting herself off the hook was a sign of weakness. The more she put in, the more she was rewarded. She controlled any variable that could interfere with her performance: her diet, her exercise, her recovery rituals, and her sleep. Very little was left to chance.

She applied similar strategies to her studies and training to become a lawyer. She studied hard and put in long hours. She revised intently and intensely. From her unpaid internship to an underpaid entry-level job, she could outwork anyone. The intrinsic hits of doing well and becoming more skilled were more than enough to build her feelings of self-worth.

Her boyfriend at the time, and now-husband, found her intensity and intellect attractive. After they married, they felt the pull to take 'the next step' and start family planning. The well-organised person that she was, Kate ensured that their finances were lined up, read the baby books, and planned for a reasonable date of when they wanted to get pregnant. She took into consideration the busy periods at the firm, financial and investment targets, and the age of her prospective child when starting school.

Kate felt good at life. She could organise it, change variables to manipulate it, and ensure security and success. At least, so she thought. Fast forward to her life as a mother of a five-year-old, eight-year-old, and eleven-year-old. Her previous tactics were not quite working for her. The more she pushed, the more she struggled.

Having learned to control her sense of worthiness through achievement, her finances through investment, and her social relationships through maintaining a delightfully 'together' facade, Kate's life experiences reinforced her deep-seated need for, and the illusion of, control.

Kate's illusion of control over her children did not take

the traditional form of policing their every move. She did not tell them what to wear; she allowed them to express themselves. She did not punish them for bad behaviour. Instead, she expressed disappointment and reminded them of positive behaviour to remember for next time. They valued emotional literacy and implemented the language of social skill programs within the home. She was warm but firm, at least in front of other parents. She ensured that they did their homework, followed the family schedule, completed their daily chores, partook in extra-curricular activities including sports, scheduled regular play dates, and read with them every night.

Kate mapped out the facets of their life. She ticked the boxes one by one, preparing her children for the competitive world. She was driven by a well-intended desire for them to have a happy and successful life. She loved them so deeply and wanted to equip them with everything she could to reduce their chances of suffering by increasing their resilience, in the best way that she knew how. When her family was happy, she was happy enough. The invisible illusion of control that Kate experienced was parenting perfectionism. If she performed as a parent to a certain level, she would not have to face the discomfort of the shame or guilt of being an imperfect parent.

They had everything they ever needed and wanted. They lived in a nice home, were financially stable, and had a full social life. Yet she buried a lingering sense that everything she had was still not enough; something was missing. Would she ever be happy with this constant yearning for more? More children, more money, more investments, more nice clothes, more books, more educational toys, and more activities. Ironically, *more* coincided with feelings of not-enoughness—internal emptiness.

Kate had spent most of her life and parenthood reaching and grasping for joy, contentment, and fulfilment, yet she was seemingly unable to fully achieve it. Falling short of her unrealistic standards, she experienced low self-esteem and features of major depressive disorder. Although she was able to hide it well, behind her nice clothes, red lipstick, and confident demeanour, at times, she experienced suicide ideation. She did not want to end her life. In fact, she was embarrassed about such fleeting thoughts. But the inability to live up to her expectations left her feeling inadequate and snowballed into all areas of her life. The external façade of her life was the epitome of 'perfection', while internally, she was falling apart. And yet, she was too stubborn to accept the help that she needed.

THE WISDOM OF CHILDREN

Many of us are shaped to believe that there is a bulletproof checklist that we can use to ensure our children's future success. We give them the best education. We make sure they develop numerous abilities and skills from the earliest age. We overfill their schedules so that they are always learning and being productive in the name of 'opportunity' and 'resilience'. True resilience is paramount. However, it has become another buzzword for a benchmark that we try to achieve. More often than not, the concept of building resilience in children is mistaken for dismissing a child's emotions, with a nudge towards toughening up. This counts as an emotional connection miss, which is counterproductive to the development of their inner emotional resources.

A striving approach to parenting is similar to the way in which we strive in our own lives: if I do this now, I will guarantee that later. Or similarly, if I achieve this now, I can avoid that later. Of course, there are many practical situations where this approach can work. If we save and invest money now, we are likely to have more later. However, this assumption of cause and effect is not guaranteed. Many people live their entire lives believing that if they prioritize their achievements now, they will find happiness later. But later never seems to come.

We unconsciously fall into the same trap with parenting. If we tell them the lessons of life now, they will know them later. If we teach children about resilience, they will be able to handle whatever comes their way in the future. If we insist that they take responsibility for their behaviour, they will become functioning citizens. But the idea that we can discipline children now, so they develop resilience later, can still function under our illusion of control. Using the law of cause and effect to parent a child can reinforce cycles of disconnection. The only way we can help children develop genuine resilience is by relating to them in the present moment.

As humans, we are a time-travelling, future-oriented species. Most of us live our days as parents, and ultimately, our lives anywhere but in the present. We parent infants so they become capable toddlers, then shape toddlers to be capable children, then prepare children to be capable adolescents, so then they can become happy adults. Preparing for the next developmental stage is a natural part of human development. But the more intelligent we become as a collective species, the more we strive for preparedness. We plan, analyse, strategise, manipulate variables, read the books, and do the courses in a state of striving for constant personal and professional improvement.

When I take on a new parent–child client duo, I meet with the parent first. At the end of the session, I ask them the miracle question, 'If you could snap your fingers to help your child, what exactly would you like to see changed?' Regardless of the reason for their referral, education level, or socioeconomic status, the answers almost always hover around the exact same themes: resilience, self-regulation, and of course, happiness. The answers usually sound something like this: 'I want them to develop resilience so they are more resilient in the future and can cope in the world. I want them to be able to manage their anxiety and emotional outbursts better, and really deep in my heart, I just want them to be happy, so they have a happy life.'

Prior to attending in person, the same parents have usually completed an intake form where they write down the perceived issues they need help with. These issues are usually some combination of childhood anxiety, sleeping issues, possible depression, low self-esteem, extreme emotional outbursts, disrespectful behaviour, impulsivity, defiance, authority issues, and behaviour problems.

I spend the second session with the child. From the way the parents have described them, I might imagine meeting a child with a myriad of psychological symptoms and difficulties. But the child who walks into the room seems very, well, normal. Sharing these insights highlight an interesting observation that presents itself again and again.

As it's natural to feel nervous with a new person, especially a new adult in a new place, the main focus of the session is to help the child feel comfortable. Towards the end, I ask them, 'If we could wave a magic wand over your life and grant you three wishes to make it easier, happier, or more meaningful, what would you wish for?' Sometimes, their answers are cheeky. They wish for what many adults would probably say, too: a million dollars, a Ferrari, a bigger house with a pool, or a holiday to Hawaii, with unlimited ice cream. Their real answers are incredibly wise: I want to feel less anxious and more confident in myself; I want to stop getting in trouble and make better choices; I want a better relationship with my family; I want to make more friends; I want to sleep better at night without needing mum or dad so I can have sleepovers with my friends. Many sensitive children dedicate one wish to the world: I wish that everyone would be nicer to each other, that bullies didn't exist, or that everyone could just get along.

Then I ask them, 'If we could wave this wand over your parents to change something about them, what would it be?' Their responses might shock you. 'I wish that my parents would stop yelling at me. I wish they listened to me more and took my opinion seriously. I wish I had more one-on-one time with mum or dad. I wish we could spend more time together as a family.'

Their answers, 100 percent of the time, revolve around being felt, seen, heard, and respected, not just as a child but as a person.

These patterns provide profound insight. If you compare the parent's intentions for the child and the child's emotional and developmental needs, the parent's intentions are more often oriented in a future result for their child. Yet when the child identifies what they need from the parent, it is always grounded in the present—what they need *now*.

This belief that if we push children to launch, they will fly later, is not serving our children or us. We know, deep down, the children are right. Emotional growth starts in the present.

THE ILLUSION OF CONTROL

Most of our suffering is the result of our illusions of control. These illusions are invisible to us because they are societally accepted as the norm. In the case of Kate, she constructed her life in such a way that if her kids failed to thrive, no one could blame her parenting ability. Her children could never make her feel ashamed, because she could show them every box that she ticked for them. Most importantly, she could never perceive herself as anything less than an incredible parent, because she did everything by the book. She taught them morals, values, and discipline. She felt relief when each day met her expectations: the kids were dressed in clean clothes, they ate a nutritious breakfast, they cleaned up their toys, and they were ready to leave on time. They used their manners, they followed the schedule, and they did things to make her proud in an attempt to please her. However, the one thing that she wasn't able to do was to free herself of the rigid rules that ran her life.

She was a slave to her perfectionism, as many of us are, and as a result, she experienced very little genuine joy. She even believed that it was normal to sacrifice her own well-being, vitality, and pleasure for her children. The cycle of control in life and parenting is the result of what psychologists refer to as psychological rigidity.

In acceptance and commitment therapy (ACT), psychological rigidity is the basis that underlies suffering and poor psychological well-being. A definition that encapsulates the experience of Kate is a state of not being present, loss or diminished connection with what matters (our values), fusing with storylines about the self, and attempts to control, alter, or avoid certain private events, especially distressing ones.[4]

In order to feel happy, we try hard to control what we're feeling by getting rid of bad feelings. This perpetual cycle, built through ineffective control strategies, is what Russ Harris coined as The Happiness Trap.[5] The problem is that the harder we try to be happy, the more unpleasant feelings we create. Psychological rigidity predicts many psychological disorders, which explains why mindfulness-based interventions that enhance our psychological flexibility, such as ACT, are effective for individuals with a range of symptoms, including anxiety and depression.[6] It is also not surprising that many studies report how enhanced psychological flexibility is helpful for parents.[7] Rigidity reinforces the framing of control, stress, perfectionism, and ultimately, depletion.

As a society, we keep going around in full circles, each decade with a slightly different flavour of control. To be perfect. To be good enough. To be the new perfect, which is a little bit vulnerable, but not too vulnerable. We are masters at masking our parenting perfectionism. We feel so judged by others, so we judge them, and they judge us, and then we judge them for judging us. We place our inherent worthiness on our external achievements and wear how busy we are as a status symbol. We justify our unhappiness with the idea that we will be happy when… we will feel grateful when…we will experience joy when… we can be present when…but the *when* never comes.

Striving for happiness is another illusion of cause and effect. If our children are unhappy now, it is acceptable so long as we ensure that they can be happy later. In my clinical work and research with families, I get to work across different generations, from screening infants for autism to working with young adults, parents, and even grandparents. It is incredibly insightful to work with three generations from one family and observe the common themes that present. The happiness trap can get passed down from generation to generation. Children start to imitate the psychological rigidity of their parents, which is another source of stress and responsibility for the parents too.

It's not our fault we fall under this illusion. Even the most conventional parenting definitions are future-achievement and control oriented. We feel that we must mould our child with desired traits to prove our competence as parents. For example, many definitions include an aspect of raising a child to maturity with competence and self-esteem. The list goes on: to ensure our child has emotional intelligence, social skills, manners, areas of excellence, sporting ability, a creative flair, and a life purpose. Instead, we should more simply redefine parenting as the process of fully meeting our child in the present moment.

The present is the only place where we can truly connect, bond, attach, play, and experience shared joy and gratitude. There would also be some fine print: parenting means to love unconditionally, which means pain, suffering, and risk of emotional exposure and possible rejection. Also known as vulnerability. There will be pain regardless, but we suffer less when we accept and make space for difficult emotions and unpleasant experiences.

CHAPTER 3

Mind: Stories about the Self

'I'm so tired. Why is this so hard? I don't know if I should have even had kids... What kind of mother would even think that? What is wrong with me? I'm definitely going to mess these kids up.'

There is a part of the mind that is a never-ending commentator. When things are going well for us, this internal commentator may be nice: a beautiful soothing voice, reminding us of all the things that we're doing right. And then, in the blink of an eye, the channel changes to the world-is-ending news. We hear a recap of all the horrible things that we have ever done and all the ways our life is lacking. Regardless of which channel is on, we are always telling ourselves stories. Good, bad, and ugly.

We mindlessly think in stories without realising this internal chatter is constant, all day and sometimes all night. It's often so mindless, that we don't even realise we have an internal commentator feeding us observations and memories of the past, predicting the future, making judgements about ourselves and others, and monitoring how we act. Who should we listen to: the nice inner commentator or the mean one? Perhaps neither.

We all mistake the voice of the commentator for our own voice. Let's introduce a case study to create some context. Emma loves being a mother but constantly feels stressed and anxious. When we first met, I asked her to tell me about herself.

> I am a mother of two children, a fur baby, and a wife to Tom. I have been a nurse for fifteen years, and I love my job. If I could do anything, I would be an artist. I love being a mother, but it's so tiring and I feel constantly exhausted. Someone always needs me, and I have no time to do anything that I want to do. I am always saying or doing the wrong thing, but I've always been awkward and anxious. I don't have much confidence in myself because I was bullied at school. I still have trouble concentrating and have always wondered if I have ADHD. I don't know though. It might just be anxiety because I didn't have a great upbringing. That's why it is so important to me that I am a great mother and I give my boys the best opportunities in life.

Like most people, Emma has a convincing story about who she is and how she landed there. When Emma was asked to describe herself, she told me the roles she plays (mother, wife, nurse), descriptions of the problems she is experiencing (tired, exhausted, anxious, awkward, distracted), and the way she makes sense of her life circumstances (victim of bullying, possible trauma, her upbringing). She considers her true self an artist.

After reviewing her story, I asked Emma, 'If this story is who you are, then it must have been true since birth.' After all, she did say that she was forty years old. When we looked back on her story, she could see that all of these things were descriptions of what she does, how she perceives herself, and the way that she has made sense of her life. We worked backwards by asking these questions: Who were you before you were a mother? Who were you before you were a nurse? Who were you before you were bullied? Who were you before you had a poor upbringing? Who were you before you developed language and identified with your internal commentator?

She was initially confused and frustrated. More therapist crap. And then there was an aha moment. Given her brain has grown and every cell has replaced itself to reform since birth to this moment, she is not her brain or mind itself. She started to recognise an aspect of the transcendent self—a part of the mind that is always there regardless of our stories, the contents of our thoughts, and the tone of the commentator.

The next step for Emma was to get some distance from her thoughts and stories by taking a more flexible perspective. The way she did this was by adding, 'I notice that I think I am...' to her self-descriptions; 'I notice that I am labelling the reaction or sensation as...' to her self-judgements; and 'I notice that the way I make sense of my story is by...' Let's consider her new story.

> I notice that I think I am a mother of two children, a fur baby, and a wife to Tom. I notice that I think I was a nurse for fifteen years. I notice that I love my job, but if I could do anything, I notice that I think I would be an artist. I notice that I love being a mother, but I notice that I am labelling the reaction or sensation as being tired and constantly exhausted. I notice that the way I make sense of my story is by feeling like someone always needs me and I have no time to do anything I want to do. I notice that I am labelling my reaction as being anxious, awkward, and lacking confidence. I notice that the way I make sense of my story is because of my upbringing and being bullied as a child. I notice that I am labelling my sensation as having poor concentration, and I notice that I am making sense of this because of possible ADHD.

Emma's new story is a little uncomfortable to read, yet

it's slightly more accurate. As you can see, most if not all of our self-image and the stories we tell about ourselves are completely made up. You might be thinking, 'But these facts are true... She does have two children...she is a mother...she is a wife,' etc. Well, there is an abundance of facts that she has left out: she is Australian, she is a fruit eater, she listens to classical music to relax. They are just descriptions. If who Emma was came down to those facts—being a mother, wife, and nurse—then who was she *before* she gained those titles? Did she have a mind, body, and soul before she was a mother, wife, and nurse? In that case, who was she then?

Our self-descriptions are influenced by our perception, our emotional responses, and how we have interpreted that situation in context. That's why two people can go through the exact same experience and have completely different interpretations. The difference is usually the result of the emotions attached to the experience, and if we were able, we could lean towards them and allow them to be felt and processed.

When Emma was bullied, she suppressed and numbed her feelings because she did not have an emotionally safe environment to express, regulate, and co-regulate in her home environment. Emma's friend, Mary, was also bullied by the same children. However, she had an entirely different experience, and it is not attached to her life story of who she is, partly because she had resources around her to turn towards. At the time, Emma was considered the 'resilient' one. She could pick herself up and go to school again and again. Mary looked like she was the one who was most affected, the one who was not coping. Their teacher thought Mary 'lacked resilience'. Mary was healthily expressing her emotions, and Emma had learnt to mask them. However, it's the suppressing of emotions that leads to trauma responses, not the expression of emotions.

The confusion around true resilience and healthy emotional expression is very much a problem today. I often receive referrals for children from doctors, teachers, and parents with complaints such as 'low resilience when her father yells at her' or she needs to come to therapy to 'increase her resilience'. The first describes a child who was being verbally abused by a parent; the second is a child who was being emotionally manipulated in her environment. I have always felt both cautious and uncomfortable around the language of raising 'resilient' children for this reason. More often than not, it is a way to distract from the environmental problems, and it overemphasises the adaptation of the child.

It is natural and healthy for children to feel anxious when they are screamed at. They are not meant to accept fault and move on calmly—especially when they are being shamed or unfairly addressed—but that is what we often expect of them. When we overlook what is really happening in their environment, we force them to build their self-image and stories of who they are around external problems that have little to do with the true nature of who they are.

OUR SELF CONSTRUCT GETS IN OUR WAY

The way we view ourselves is constructed throughout our lives. It is sometimes referred to as the conceptualised self, or more commonly referred to in layman terms as the ego. Similar to resilience, the ego is often misunderstood in the mainstream. If we asked a random group of people on the street what it means if someone has an ego, the answers would probably hover around the theme of arrogance, narcissism, or an overly inflated sense of entitlement. However, the true essence of the ego that emerges from Freud's psychoanalytic work is that it is a normal part of the human psyche.

The ego works as an unconscious mediator that acts as a protector between our need for pleasure or avoidance of discomfort and our need to conform to societal expectations. The way we conform is shaped by our self-image (the story of who we are and what makes us worthy) and our innate human need for social belonging (whatever we need to do to feel like a worthy part of the group). The more rigidly attached we are to our 'I' stories and self-image—our self-descriptions, judgements, sense of worthiness, and identity within our group—the more vulnerable we become to living a life of social conformity.

To take ownership over our lives, we have to evaluate how the role of conformity and pleasing others' expectations—real or perceived—impacts our relationship with ourselves. This will allow us to step back and gain distance from the stories that make up our thought patterns and to simply learn to observe them. We don't need to try to positively think our way around the image of who we are and how we should behave. We benefit from just bringing awareness to these patterns. This is the reason why we cannot positively think our way out of trauma, low self-esteem, stress, anxiety, depression, or really anything else. And the truth is that we don't have to. There is another way that is more effective.

Just as an exercise to elaborate on the limitations of fixating on our self-stories, I asked Emma to tell me all of the positive things about herself to try to build her self-esteem. Her responses were, 'I am a good mother, I am a good wife, I am good at drawing, I am a nice person, I am a really good friend, and I think I am a good nurse.'

I respond, 'So you're saying that you're good at everything that makes you who you are. Why do you think you still have low self-esteem? Do you need to be better at more things to be good enough?' She looked a little confused. I enquired further, 'Are you good at those things consistently, all of the time?' She shook her head. She seemed to start to really take in the limitations of her self-descriptions.

She started to realise that no matter what she does, she cannot find a way to sustain her feelings of being good enough. One of the most important parts of her conceptualised identity—that how she feels makes her life worth living—is being the great mother that she never had. Yet when our sense of self is over-reliant on 'achieving' as a mother, our natural parenting abilities start to reduce. This happens because without even realising it, there is too much at stake for us.

Let's say that Emma's son experiences insomnia. He is emotionally overwhelmed and overtired, and starts having frequent outbursts that are mostly saved for home. Because Emma is his primary attachment figure, he loses control of his emotions around her. This is understandably exhausting for Emma, and she becomes increasingly reactive. Her internal commentator is scanning through all options. What's wrong with his behaviour? Maybe it's anxiety? She had a bad feeling about his teacher. Maybe she passed on her ADHD to him and something has just triggered it? She goes into commentator/analyser mode.

One night, she sits down with her son to talk about his

worries. He says he is uncomfortable telling her, but he will write them down—'there's too much pressure on me, I feel like I am not smart enough, I'm always getting in trouble, no one listens to me at home'. Emma's heart is racing. She feels a combination of guilt, denial, and rage. She responds, 'Honey, you know that's not true' and goes into dismissing, defending, and disqualifying mode. She does everything to explain to him why those worries are irrational and invalid, offering some suggestions of more positive thoughts to think.

When Emma goes to bed, she ruminates on what happened and draws on memories to put together a theory to explain her son's behaviour. When her son went to bed feeling confused, he was still anxious but trying to think happy thoughts. Over time, he started to seem better but was a little spaced out and detached from his emotions. Emma thought maybe her pep talks at night were helping him to see that his perspective was irrational. She had convinced him that her experienced adult perspective was more accurate and that he would learn to make better choices and develop resilience. So how did Emma's story of needing to be a great mother get in the way in this example? As she unconsciously flew into disqualifying and need-to-fix mode, she missed an opportunity to actively listen, help him to identify and regulate his *emotions*, and hold space for him to reframe his own story about what was happening for him. This example is subtle, but common and important.

This is what a lot of people mean when they refer to doing the 'inner work' as a parent. We start by becoming more aware of the commentator and how the ego constructs the stories of our mind, acting like an algorithm. This algorithm is dictated by a number of rules to protect our self-image. Some psychologists refer to these rules as core beliefs. If you have the rule that 'good mothers stay at home with their kids', your ego is going to take you on a wild ride when you want to go back to work. This process often works beyond our conscious awareness. That's why we can deny our own reality, or the reality of others. We lie to ourselves and to others when something doesn't fit in our conceptualised reality, because we need to protect this perception as a survival mechanism.

Our ego is driven by social and psychological survival, which can often play out as people pleasing, conforming, only remembering aspects of a situation, rejecting shameful parts of ourselves, and doing whatever needs to be done to protect and control how others perceive us. It can be threatened just by perception alone. For example, say you view yourself as being highly educated in a particular area, and then you hear a colleague discussing something that you didn't already know. You go along with it at the time and act like you knew about it already. Yet internally, you feel emotionally triggered. On the way home, you feel a bit deflated and notice the commentator adding some notes, 'I guess you're not that much of an expert after all...'

which equates to, 'They must think you're dumb.' As you have a rise of uncomfortable and anxious emotions, the protective mechanisms start by mentally poking holes in your colleague's story, judging them as being a know-it-all.

Okay, now apply this experience to motherhood and double—or triple—the emotional intensity. Parenting can give rise to enormous defensive work of the ego, especially when we are trying to maintain our identity of being a really good or perfect parent. Many conscientious parents—myself included—highly value showing up as the best parent they can be. The ego dance is performed when we place external contingencies upon our perceived success: how others view us, how well our children present, and how our family looks to others. The activation of the ego is reflected in the internal commentary and reasoning process that can occur simply after we have perceived a triggering comment.

For example, imagine your mother's group is talking about a new parenting book and an approach called 'conscious parenting'. They are talking about which child is their biggest 'trigger child' and 'spiritual teacher'. The internal commentator is very sceptical and in a hypervigilant state. 'Did someone just say the word *soul*? It all sounds very woo-woo. If their kids are spiritual teachers, they should take in my kids for one day. I'm sure that will knock some sense into them and their crystals.'

That night you tell your husband that you're not going to continue going to the mother's group. You justify that it's because they're not really your people, you're not really clicking with them, and they're a bit judgemental. When the ego is threatened, we project that we do not belong, and defence mechanisms take over the ability to make flexible, conscious choices.

PARENTING BEYOND PSYCHOLOGICAL RIGIDITY

We have a natural resistance to relate differently to our rules and self-image because we think we don't know who we are without them. I have learnt a lot from Shefali Tsabary on how the ego plays out in parenting.[8] While reading her book *The Conscious Parent* for the first time, I had an inner knowing that she was describing patterns that I was observing in my life and psychology practice. She contrasts parenting from a place of ego with parenting from our own wounds instead of from our wholeness. She emphasises that we are rarely not driven by our ego when it comes to parenting our children. We consider them as an extension of ourselves, from the very way we describe them as 'my children' to how personally we take how they perform at school, how they look, who they marry, where they live, and what they do for a living. From preconception to years later, we usually bring some sense of fantasy to what our children will be like. I am consciously aware of this, and still, I catch myself falling into these traps, even in subtle ways.

Emma's interactions with her son demonstrate how we can become so fixated on the description and stories of situations with an emphasis on their validity, instead of being focussed on connection and emotion. For example, instead of connecting 'you seem really tired and overwhelmed' and then validating, 'a few deep breaths and a good night's sleep can help when you have so many big feelings', she reverted to 'that's not true'. What is said in these examples is nowhere near as important as what is felt. We can be so desperate for children to see our reality, and in the process, we unconsciously teach them to reject their emotional experiences. If we don't know what to say, we can always just come back to exploring how they are feeling. Most of what children need from us is freely available—our presence, our eye contact, our attunement, and our compassion towards their perspective and experience. Parenting children to conform to our expectations of how we should be as parents and how they should act as children guarantees reactive parenting patterns.

Common ways to identify when we are rigidly reacting to our children is when we experience a knee-jerk response and fall into domination, righteousness, and control. On these inevitable occasions, we can start to shift our line of thinking by asking ourselves empowering questions. For example, when Sarah from Chapter 1 was at her son Oliver's door in the morning, she asked herself, 'Why won't he listen? How can I control his behaviour? Is it my fault?

What's wrong with him? Why isn't he like other kids?' And so on. Only with the skills to overcome our illusions of power and conformity can we fully meet our children with an attitude of non-judgemental and conscious awareness. Some empowering questions that facilitate a more flexible inquiry for Sarah may be: How can I work through my own triggers when I am around him? How am I contributing to the ongoing power struggle? What are other possible factors that make him not want to get out of bed? Could there be an unaddressed or unresolved issue that I am not aware of? How could we give him a stronger sense of autonomy but still set limits around going to school?

She may have discovered some contributing factors that had very little to do with her parenting and were more related to the relationship they had. Yet, her fixation on his compliance, in order to confirm her competence as a mother, created a barrier between them. By asking more empowering questions—those that enquire about breaking the cycle rather than perpetuating the cycle—she would have been better able to be there for him. She may have learnt that he was struggling academically and socially while attending a high-achieving, sporty, all-boys school. With more personal strengths and talents in artistic and creative endeavours, his individuation was not supported in his environment.

When a school psychologist mentioned to Sarah and her

husband that their son appeared withdrawn and was experiencing symptoms of depression, they were shocked. Their reactive question was, 'What did we do wrong?' Their empowering question was, 'How can we better understand how he's feeling?' Shifting our enquiry from focussing on our experience to our child's experience is the best way to repair the parent–child relationship. This attunement requires continuous work. As our children grow, we must learn to reattune to them at each developmental phase.

As they practised being more present with him, active listening, and connecting to his emotions, over time, they started to understand his internal world. Oliver spent his weekends trying to improve his sporting ability to fit in more at school, but he still reported that he felt no sense of competence in pretty much any area of his life. He made comments alluding to the fact that he was struggling with his sexuality but could not bear the thought of being even more different than his peers. He already felt that he did not belong. Yet, through the process of strengthening the parent–child relationship, he began to feel a greater sense of belonging at home: a lifeline for a struggling adolescent.

Learning to become less rigid in our reactions largely depends on our own set of psychological flexibility skills that can be learned and practised. It involves working on our tendency to react on autopilot with rigidity and stepping back to observe the antics of the internal commentator. When we learn to develop a more flexible self-image, it helps us to become more responsive and flexible as a person and therefore as a parent.

In the next chapter, we will explore how psychological rigidity works by default and why practising mindfulness can free us from the stories we tell ourselves. This transformation isn't something that occurs overnight as an awakening. It is the process of noticing more in daily life: small shifts from mindlessness to mindfulness, from distraction to presence, to being the internal commentator to observing the internal commentator. The transcendent self that has many street names—the true self, the authentic self, the higher self—is experienced in glimpses of being present with total awareness.

CHAPTER 4

Unconscious: Default to Awareness

Imagine a group of researchers scanned your brain while you were sitting and waiting. You were instructed to do nothing and rest. What do you think the researchers would find?

1. **A doing-attention state:** mind-wandering, mindless scrolling, making judgements about being bored, thinking about the past, and planning for the future.
2. **A being-attention state:** resting in the here and now with an attention focal point on the senses, the body, or the breath.

Next, you were asked to switch your attention from rest to engage with a cognitive task. Say you were playing a game of Kahoot! where you need to pay attention to the instruction and respond promptly. What do you think the brain scans would show?

1. You could not switch your attention to engage in the game at all.
2. You were able to switch your attention from mind-wandering to focus, able to bring your attention fully to the task, showing a difference in your brain between rest and the cognitive task.
3. As you were resting with full-focussed attention in the present, when you switched to the task, there was probably not a notable difference in the brain.

Third, imagine you were to sustain your attention on the game for a longer period of time. Instead of playing one fifteen-minute game, you were to play three fifteen-minute games. What do you think your brain scan would show?

1. Mindlessly tuning out after the first game, unable to sustain attention on the task.
2. Involuntary switching from paying full attention to mind-wandering throughout each game where you consciously bring your attention back to the task.
3. Sustained and focussed attention to the cognitive task for most of the three games.

I suspect the most common responses would be 1-2-2. This

result would suggest that when you are not consciously engaged in a task, the default mode network in the brain is activated. The default network consists of a series of brain regions that co-activate when we are not paying attention. It is shown to activate on brain scans when our mind is wandering, lost in thought, and running on autopilot. An example of this may be when we go through the motions of our usual routine—get dressed, have breakfast, drive to work, and end up sitting at our desk with little recollection of the morning. We didn't really taste the food, pay attention to which way we drove, or notice our surroundings on the way. We are often *mindless* when doing familiar and mundane tasks. The default mode network is often activated when we are in a doing-attention state. In contrast, the being-attention state is synonymous with mindfulness.

STRENGTHENING PATHWAYS TO SUSTAIN ATTENTION

A recent study was published in late 2020 in Japan where researchers scanned the brains of participants during a rest state, while attention-switching from rest to task, and while sustaining attention to task.[9] They found that psychological resilience was associated with dynamic changes in the patterns of the default mode network during the cognitive task. The researchers found that in individuals with higher resilience, their default mode patterns were more stable in the face of cognitive demand. For the purposes of making their findings relatable, we could hypothesise that those who answered 2-3-3 in the previous exercise would show more stable patterns in the brain, reflecting higher psychological resilience.

To improve our psychological resilience, or psychological well-being overall, we can train our attention to reduce the amount of time we unconsciously mind-wander and activate default mode. There is an old saying in neuroscience that what fires together, wires together. This is especially true for this network of brain function: the more we are in default mode, the stronger it becomes in our automatic baseline state. It is natural to automatically shift into default mode, but as a generalisation, the more we are consciously aware, the better our psychological health will be. The more we wire our brain for presence, attention, connection, and self-regulation, the stronger these traits become as our upgraded baseline state.

By developing self-awareness, we can start to recognise when we go into autopilot and develop our attention skills to be able to reconnect with the present. There is a substantial body of research that has found that the more time the default mode network in our brain is activated, the more likely we are to experience a myriad of mental health problems, including stress, anxiety, depression, and many other psychological symptoms. One of the main by-products of default mode that weakens our mental health and well-being is the tendency to ruminate.[10]

All of us can likely recognise a time where we have gone over and over something in our mind, be it replaying a situation that occurred in the past or projecting scenarios about the future. In default mode, we can be psychologically rigid and get stuck on these repetitive thoughts, which is usually parallel with negative and self-critical thoughts. Rumination is strongly associated with depressive episodes and can predict the onset and duration of depressive cycles.[11] It is likely the most essential single factor in developing depression or relapsing into a depressive state.

We often unconsciously lose our precious rejuvenation time to default mode when we are scrolling, commuting, watching TV, with family and friends, and on holidays. Yet, those who bring deliberate attention to rest and recreation are likely to actually receive more benefits—from improved relationships to better quality rest and recovery. The subtle shifts in everyday life can be as simple and significant as putting your phone out of reach while watching a movie so you can fully focus on the movie. Instead of getting hooked on stories about work, it might mean *fully* listening to music on your commute and genuinely enjoying the tune. Sadly, many people spend a large amount of their time with loved ones—partners and children included—in a default state. It's very easy to fall victim to this without effortful awareness as we move through the motions getting dinner on the table, the house in order, kids bathed and in bed, along with everything that comes in between.

When it comes to parenting, being trapped in the cycle of default mode means we are most likely subject to reactive parenting patterns, which makes us set up to fail. We may have an idea about how to best parent our children, but ultimately, our reactions are shaped by the baseline of our brain. We have much less conscious choice than we think without doing the 'inner work' to observe our patterns and develop greater self-awareness.

Something that is important to acknowledge is that unaddressed, untreated, and unprocessed trauma from our past or childhood may be contributing to our inability to live in the present. While there are vast differences between simple (an event or series of relatively minor events) and complex developmental (relatively ongoing abuse, neglect, etc. from childhood) trauma, many of us have had experiences that were somehow or somewhat traumatic at the time. This could be any experience where we were 'flooded' (unable to cope), because we did not have the psychological resources or environmental supports to fully process the emotional impact at the time.

Our understanding of how trauma affects the mind and body continues to sophisticate with new research findings. This body of work would be incomplete without acknowledging that our default mode network could be altered by trauma from the past, making it quite challenging to live with presence. We are often unconscious as to how trauma impacts our world today. We are often unconscious as to how these patterns shape our parenting today, especially if we have not processed trauma or dysfunctional patterns that were shaped from our childhood.

To address trauma, there usually needs to be a trio of mind–body integration in therapy to support the nervous system. This may involve trauma-informed therapy that addresses the past (for example, Eye-Movement Desensitisation Therapy; EMDR), attention and emotion regulation in the present, and the regulation of the autonomic nervous system. To understand how some of our own parenting patterns can be shaped by the past, we are going to explore how our schemas or mental shortcuts unconsciously guide our behaviour.

DEFAULT PARENTING SCHEMAS

Have you ever reacted to your children unintentionally and paused with a slight panic realisation that in that moment you sounded a lot like your mother? Most people I have met in clinical practice would not describe this as a compliment. It seems natural that people desire to do better than their parents, even with the awareness that most people genuinely do the best they can with the resources they have at the time. It's also understandable given how much the psychology of parenting has evolved. Our grandparents and parents could not have possibly known what we now know about emotional development, social intelligence, and the importance of emotion-focussed parenting. Thankfully, with this new knowledge, the way we discipline children has evolved away from cold and harsh discipline. Although in one way it feels like ancient knowledge, it really wasn't all that long ago that Oprah was discussing why you shouldn't smack children on her show, leaving many well-meaning parents confused as to how to discipline and teach good morals to their children. Now that we have more knowledge and awareness to improve our parenting, it is our radical responsibility to improve our actions—with self-compassion.

One of the ways that psychologists understand the cycle of parents unconsciously turning into their parents is through the concept of schemas. This understanding emerges from schema therapy, an integrative psychotherapy developed by Jeffry Young in the eighties.[12] Schemas are like a mental framework that unconsciously organises our patterns of thoughts and behaviour—like our automatic habits—that are shaped by our preconceived ideas and past experiences. Although psychologists have operationally defined different types of schemas into categories, our schemas are unique to our past and perception of the world. When we learn new information that fits into our current schemas and worldview, the more likely we are to accept this information. You may even notice an automatic rejection of new information presented in this book at times as it differs from the way you previously viewed a concept. In a way, our mental schemas can be considered the mental sets that unconsciously organise the ego: what it needs to protect and what it needs to reject to maintain our current perceived identity.

Schemas are self-protective patterns that are thought to develop due to some unmet core needs during childhood. The main core needs of a child include a sense of safety and secure attachment to others, a sense of personal identity and autonomy, consistent and age-appropriate limits from parents, the ability to play and be spontaneous, and the freedom to express feelings and needs. These core needs are excellent guideposts for our own parenting intentions. Some of the ways we develop unhelpful schemas from childhood are:

- When our needs for emotional security have not been well met and reflect a lack of attachment security.
- If we had parents who were overprotective, over-indulgent, or permissive with a lack of limits and age-appropriate boundaries.
- If we tended to absorb and internalise our parents' emotions, and imitate their attitudes or behaviours, also known as enmeshment.

- If we grew up in environments characterised by high distress, chaos, neglect, or abuse.

Given the complexity of life, I am not sure that any of us develop into adulthood without developing schemas in one way or another. Once we have developed a schema, we are usually unaware of how it influences our thoughts and actions in order to prevent—or avoid—emotional discomfort. The schema mode governs the way we react and our perception of the world. In the context of parenting, schemas often govern the way we blindly react to our children. If you're unsure of how they play out for you, bring curiosity to your most intense emotional triggers. What is your default reaction when your child is in emotional pain? What gets under your skin resulting in an adult-sized tantrum? What is it about your child that you find intolerable? What is the biggest challenge in the co-parenting relationship?

Schema modes are broken down into four main categories in schema therapy: child modes, dysfunctional coping modes, parent modes, and healthy adult modes.

You may be familiar with the term 'inner child'. The concept of adults having an inner child comes from the child schema mode. The inner child can take different forms, and we can all experience different types of inner child modes. We will explore the four main inner child modes:

the vulnerable child, the angry child, the impulsive or undisciplined child, and the healthy child modes.

The vulnerable child feels lonely, isolated, sad, misunderstood, incompetent, needy, anxious, worthless, powerless, and so on. Then there is the angry child who feels internally enraged, frustrated, and impatient because the needs of the vulnerable child are not being met. The impulsive or undisciplined ('spoiled') child often acts on their impulses with little self-control and struggles with delayed gratification, often feeling irritable, angry or frustrated when their desires and impulses are not immediately met. The healthy child is 'contented' and feels deeply loved, connected, protected, accepted, nurtured, understood and validated. This inner child strikes a balance of being autonomous, self-reliant, adaptable and spontaneous.

HOW DIFFERENT SCHEMAS IMPACT OUR PARENTING

Let's make this knowledge more digestible through a case study. Imagine Nelly grew up without solid attachment or emotional security to her parents. Her father was absent, and her mother was permissive—lacking boundaries—and acted like her best friend. When Nelly's daughter disagrees with her opinions and beliefs, Nelly is highly triggered. She unconsciously shifts into the angry child mode and rages at her daughter in order to protect her vulnerable inner child from being misunderstood. There is also an element of the impulsive and undisciplined child mode as she did not learn healthy boundaries in interpersonal relationships and how to respect different perspectives as a child. Disagreement was an unconscious threat to having her core needs met.

Nelly takes her daughter to see a psychologist because she perceives her to have such irrational beliefs about life and the world that—she perceives—need to be fixed. She struggles to sit with the discomfort of having differing opinions and does not have the mindfulness and emotion-regulation skills to bring tolerance to the experience to allow her strong emotional reactions to pass. She logically knows her reactions are extreme, but given her unconscious mode, she tends to project it to be a fault of her daughter's. Her ego is in full force to protect her familiar schemas because that was how she received love as a child. When these cycles repeat again and again over time, it's pretty clear how the ongoing ruptures deteriorate their relationship. Nelly is very well intended and loves her daughter more than anything, but she does not have the willingness, tolerance, or psychological skills to regulate her default mode and schemas—two cycles that will almost guarantee conflictual and unhealthy relationship patterns with her daughter if they remain unaddressed over the long term.

Let's explore a different manifestation of child schema

modes experienced by Kate from Chapter 2. In contrast to how Nelly was repeating a similar pattern to her parents and because Kate wanted to parent in the completely opposite way of her parents, her schema modes played out differently. Of course, the same concepts apply to fathers too.

Kate grew up in an upper-middle-class family with four siblings. They had the white picket fence family house, went to a private school, and were given plenty of 'opportunities'. She spent every night learning languages, practising musical instruments, playing a sport, or tutoring. She was expected to please her parents at all costs, which characterises a theme of emotional neglect. There was also an element of enmeshment as there was basically no space for her own individuality and autonomy within the family. The children were largely expected to become lawyers to carry the family tradition. Decades later, when her own children 'shut her out' emotionally, her vulnerable child mode is activated. Sometimes this squashes her children's autonomy without her realising, and she becomes overprotective and preoccupied with their lives. In turn, they shut her out more, which makes her feel angry, resentful, and even abandoned.

INNER PARENT MODES

Just as we have developed inner child modes, we also form

inner parent modes. These modes can drive our automatic reactions that are often noncongruent with our good intentions. We will explore the punitive parent mode and the demanding (or critical) parent mode. The punitive parent mode is characterised by the feeling that we and others deserve punishment or blame for our behaviours. This mode can be unconsciously activated when our child does something that triggers us, and we fly into blaming, punishing, or even abusive behaviours. For example, if Kate's daughter refuses to do her homework, Kate may grab her arm and drag her to her desk and threaten her not to come out of her room until it is complete. This mode can have us shift from punishing our child reactively to then later blaming ourselves and ruminating on being a bad parent.

When Kate's daughter refuses to do what she says, the punitive parent in her automatically wants to punish her. She might yell, put her down, and say things that she knows will manipulate her into feeling guilty—punishment. This makes her feel in control as an authority figure. As they are enmeshed, her daughter often ends up saying things she does not believe to please and satisfy her mother. She has learnt that her mother's emotional needs are more important than hers because guilt is used as a tool.

The demanding or critical parent mode is characterised

by the inner perfectionist or the inner critic. This mode fuels parenting perfectionism: the feeling that we should be perfect, achieve at a very high level to maintain order, and strive for high standards. This mode ensures we put others' needs before our own, behave like a perfect caretaker, and avoid wasting time. You might recall how this mode plagued Kate's parenting experience, leaving very little space for self-care, play, presence, or meaning.

When Kate perceives that her children are rejecting her, her demanding/perfectionist parent dives deeper into performing and achievement behaviours—perfectly clean house, buying flowers, and working overtime to avoid her feelings of incompetence and rejection. She punishes her children by stonewalling (ignoring) their presence until they demand her love and affection and need her again. There are so many ways these modes play out in daily life, often with multiple at play simultaneously.

Many people who can relate to perfectionism can probably relate to this demanding or critical inner parent mode in some way: our own inner perfectionist. This one has been my vice that probably anyone who knows me well enough would recognise. Although perfectionism can be glamorised, what is often less obvious is how much pain and suffering it can cause below the surface: burnout, lack of balance, taking on too much, saving behaviours, putting others' needs before our own. I have met many colleagues, psychologists, and people who work in the caring profession who are similar to me in that way. I guess our vulnerable inner children want to reassure and help heal other vulnerable inner children. I have found a very healthy balance with this schema now—as I can recognise when I am back in the water—something I doubt I would have been able to do years ago. That's not to say there aren't still elements that are unconscious to me, but due to my conscious awareness and introspective skills, I can recognise when I am falling into unhealthy patterns very quickly. I have developed skills to detangle these patterns that we will continue to break down in subsequent chapters.

This is what people mean when they reference the 'inner work'. How well do you really know yourself? How much self-awareness do you really have of your own patterns, schemas, habits, and defaults?

SHIFTING FROM DEFAULT TO META-AWARENESS

If our ego, our inner child, and our inner parent could be mapped in the brain, we would probably find them in the default mode network. In other words, our default mode network is activated when we demonstrate reactive parenting behaviours. Over the last few decades, studies have repeatedly shown that reducing our default mode in the brain increases our mindful attention in the present moment and improves our psychological health. There are a few ways to reduce this network (that don't involve consciousness-altering psychedelics). They basically all come down to attention regulation, mindfulness including mindful self-compassion, and most importantly, formal meditation practice. From a brief four to seven days of practice to eight-week meditation training programs, the magnitude of the default network has been shown to weaken. This usually coincides with reduced self-reports of stress, anxiety, depression, and other markers of poor psychological well-being.

As we engage in regular practices to reduce default modes, our tendency to ruminate is likely to decrease, and we experience less repetitive thinking about negative experiences relating to the self. This means less self-criticism and negative self-talk running the mind. One of the mechanisms behind this is meditation, which is effective in reducing our self-referential process and thinking. We become less focussed on the 'I' and the stories we hold about who we are and how others perceive us. At the same time, the functional connectivity (immediate function in the brain) changes to increase our self-awareness and awareness of others. This is often referred to as meta-awareness, which improves our ability to think flexibly and embody awareness with a non-judgemental stance. As we become less influenced by our past conditioning and unconscious schemas because our meta-awareness has improved, we become less vulnerable to slip into unconscious schema modes when navigating uncomfortable emotions.

Just from this brief explanation, you can see how changes in the default network are valuable to parenting. Even when parents want to honour their child's emotional needs, if they are trapped by their self-referencing thinking—the stories they tell themselves—and get stuck in their negative ruminations, they lose the ability to freely respond with conscious choice. I hear messages about parenting all the time that can be quite harmful. They imply that a parent is choosing to be selfish, self-absorbed, emotionally reactive, or controlling towards their child. The problem with such messages is that they are judgemental but also don't show a parent how to shift their unconscious conditioning to be able to respond in ways that they desire. This just reinforces rumination and perpetuates the cycle.

As we develop a heightened awareness of our own mental state and consciousness and learn to observe our thoughts, emotions, and perception biases, we can start to break free of these patterns. This reflects the development of meta-awareness.

PART II

Breaking Free

CHAPTER 5

Interaction: Mindful Parenting Practice

Think back to a time when you were really struggling with parenting your child. The time might be now. Imagine you were able to choose one of three free parenting courses. Consider honestly which option you would choose.

1. Improve your child's behaviour and learn practical parenting skills using positive behaviour support.
2. A mindfulness-based stress-reduction course to reduce parenting stress and improve your family's well-being.
3. A mindfulness-based positive behaviour support program to reduce parenting stress and learn practical behaviour management strategies.

When I title a workshop or course something related to

behaviour management, I tend to have a wait list. The times I have offered a mindful parenting workshop to reduce parent stress...crickets. Parents would rather actually 'learn' something related to managing the child's behaviour because they tend to view their child's behaviour as an isolated issue to be corrected. There tends to be some interest in the third option, but ironically, the more stressed parents are, the more they would rather not 'waste time' working on their own stress. Instead, they want to focus on effective behaviour management strategies for their children. The problem with this is that collectively, we do not have a good understanding of parent–child interaction. We can't effectively manage a child's behaviour without reflecting on our own triggers and reactive stress patterns.

Child psychologists see this often. Parents do not want to waste their child's therapy time on themselves. They would rather have their child in the room for the whole session. Sometimes this is out of avoidance, but mostly it is because parents believe focusing exclusively on their child would lead to the best outcome. This reflects a common misconception that parents must prioritise managing the challenging behaviour of their child—without deeper consideration of the parent–child relationship, interaction, and the environmental factors that may be contributing to the situation.

What may be more helpful is for parents to learn how to

manage their own state first and foremost, in order to be able to consciously shape the transmission that occurs within parent–child interactions. With this attitude, we can see that although behaviour management is an inevitable aspect of parenting, it is still, in essence, *reactive* and should not be the primary or only parenting strategy, skill, or focus.

Nirbhay Singh has been a major force in the field of integrating meditation and mindful parenting with positive behaviour support.[13] In his 2020 study, mothers of children with autism were randomly assigned to one of three intervention programs: a mindfulness-based program, a positive-behaviour support program, or a mindfulness-based positive-behaviour support program. The researchers investigated the effects of the different intervention programs on the mothers, including their program attendance, their meditation time, and perceived self-reported psychological stress. They also investigated the indirect effects on their children with autism by measuring the child's level of aggression, disruptive behaviour, and compliance.

The parents who experienced the greatest improvements in their stress levels—both in the short and long term—were those in the mindfulness-based positive-behaviour support program, followed by the purely mindfulness-based program. Three years later, improvements in stress had been maintained across both mindfulness-based groups, which is quite an incredible result. There were no changes in the positive-behaviour support condition. So why wouldn't our stress reduce when we learn behaviour management strategies?

I'm sure by now you have worked out that the default mode network in the brain probably has something to do with it. Here's another interesting finding: *meditation time* was a significant predictor in reducing aggressive and disruptive behaviours amongst their children. The more time parents spent meditating, the more likely their children were to listen to their mother's requests and instructions. This result suggests that the most effective way for parents to improve their child's behaviours is—wait for it—doing their own time on the meditation mat. How could this be? Meditating, instead of spending time obsessing, policing, and trying to manage their child's behaviour, leads to more positive outcomes for the whole family. Something that I take away from these results is that behaviour management—even positive-behaviour management—is far less effective when parents have undeveloped mindfulness skills.

I encourage you to think of the time meditating as time investing in circuit breaking. It's training the brain to disrupt the default mode, so when interacting with our child, our brain works with us to respond instead of to react.

Mindful parenting, enhanced by meditation, is transformational when it comes to improving the parent–child relationship, which is essential for the child's genuine resilience for the rest of their life. It is circuit breaking for today and for generations to come in the future.

NON-JUDGEMENTALLY ATTENDING TO OUR CHILD

As a starting point, most mindfulness interventions involve the introduction and practices that cultivate a beginner's mind. A beginner's mind refers to a mental position emerging from the Zen Buddhist concept, *shoshin*, where we open our awareness with a willingness to see everything as though it is the first time that we have experienced it. In this process, there is a letting go or a distance created from our preconceived ideas, judgements, expectations, opinions, and biases, which opens us up to simply notice, observe, and perceive things differently.

A way to practise a beginner's mind is to choose an activity that we do regularly and commit to seeing things as if it is our very first time. Let's say that Laura decided to practise by going on her daily walk around her neighbourhood. She starts with an intention to remove distractions (i.e., her phone) and to pay attention to her senses. She may smell the air, notice the colour of the trees, and visually scan her surroundings. When she notices a judgement, like 'this is boring', and gets the urge to grab her phone, she just untangles from the thought and gently comes back to the moment. Later that day, she practises a beginner's mind when making lunch. She takes a moment to notice the food, the bowl, the spoon, and other details she would normally miss. When she takes each bite, she notices the texture, the smell, and the taste as if she is eating for the first time.

In a textbook outlining a *Mindful Parenting* program for mental health practitioners, Susan Bögels and Kathleen Restifo introduce a well-known mindful eating exercise.[14] This involves mindfully eating a raisin while systematically noticing with full attention how it feels to hold it and what it looks like, exploring the smells, placing it in the mouth, focussing on the taste of the raisin with every bite and movement, and then experiencing the feeling of swallowing.

The authors suggest adopting a similar mindful stance to a beginner's mind in parenting moments with children, calling the exercise 'child as raisin'. Parents are instructed to observe their child with full attention, as if they are seeing them for the first time, in a moment where the child is not aware that the parent is watching. This exercise helps us tune in to the beauty and impermanence of children who are ever changing. We will not experience them as they are right now in the exact same way ever again. This is a practical way to integrate a foundational aspect of mindful parenting into our lives, starting in the very next moment that we lay our eyes on our children.

One of my first mindfulness teachers described a powerful example of a little girl holding up her painting. She is excited and says, 'Mummy, look!' Her mum looks up in acknowledgement while she is sending an email and says, 'Wow, honey. That is amazing!' The girl drops her head and says, 'But you didn't even look.' Her mum responds, 'I did honey, it's beautiful.' They *know*. Children know when we aren't really listening, looking, or attending.

In addition to her son, Emma from Chapter 3 also has a primary-aged daughter. Lucy is very intelligent—almost too intelligent for her own good—and also incredibly anxious. Communicating with her felt like conversing with a much older child. If anyone surrendered to their preconceived expectations of how old she was chronologically, she would assert with a demand for respect, 'Why are you speaking to me like a baby?' Emma and her husband found her complex and manipulative. They often reacted to her by reminding her of her age and place in the family by resorting to the statement, 'You're just a kid.' When we discussed how she was feeling unheard in her family, her parents responded, 'OK, tell me more. I'm listening now. Go. What do you want me to hear?' in the tone of the eye roll. She would say how she felt, and her mum would say, 'And I hear you, Lucy!' Lucy responded, 'But you're not even listening!' And she was right. Her parents didn't seem to know *how* to listen for the intent of listening to hear, not to respond.

One of the most important, foundational skills of good communication and helping is what we refer to in counselling as active listening. Active listening is a skill that involves listening with all the senses—to fully and consciously concentrate on what is being said—which involves hearing the whole verbal and nonverbal, overt and covert message that is being shared. Only when we practise active listening can we respond to our child walking in the door, with rosy and flustered cheeks to scream in our face, 'I hate you', and have the ability to mindfully pause before reacting with a louder voice and to instead respond, 'You seem overwhelmed.'

Mindful listening involves mindful attending to what is being communicated beyond the context of words and tone of voice. It's attending to the whole being of the child without getting hooked by judgements or emotional reactions. In this example, instead of getting swept away by our punitive parent mode, we could attend to them more skilfully. For example, a punitive parent response would sound like, 'You're so disrespectful... Go to your room.' The earlier we catch the true message behind their outburst, the less chaos there will be. This is not to say that we should never use consequences for disrespectful behaviour. However, the more attuned we are to our children, the clearer we can understand their needs and respond proportionately. This will naturally reduce the use of disciplinary consequences in the first place.

The ordinary, mundane moments and repetitive tasks that make up parenting, such as bathing, feeding, preparing for naps, getting ready for school, cooking, eating dinner, reading the bedtime story, and so on, are tasks that are often rushed through to achieve the end goal—to finish the day and get everything done. In the process, we miss hundreds of effortless moments for presence and connection. We forget to make eye contact, to savour the smells, to enjoy the cuddles and shared smiles. We forget that parenting children consists of millions of seemingly mundane moments that are what shape our child above and beyond the two hours of 'quality family time' that we set aside on the weekend. Mindful parenting affords the opportunity to bring more quality to the moments that we often miss at the expense of going through the motions with doing attention. When we miss being present in an intimate cuddle, we will never have the same cuddle in the exact same way. But if we can learn to move through our day with more ease, presence, and flow, we can savour each moment.

Mindfulness becomes a way of life, and a way of parenting, that we can come back to, moment by moment, by using our senses. It may mean really feeling the water as you bathe your toddler or bringing your awareness to the feeling of the touch of a cuddle after work. It may mean listening—really listening—on the car ride home from school without interrupting, passing judgement, talking on the phone, or lecturing. If it is your intention to become more mindful as a parent, it may be helpful to first consider what your motivation is. For example, if 'connection' or 'showing up' for parenting is a core value to you, it will help you to make this way of interacting a priority. When I ask parents what the costs of absentmindedness, default mode, and general *mindlessness* are, they usually say things like:

- The time just passes so quickly. They are growing up so fast.
- I feel like I have missed so many precious moments.
- I spend most of my energy keeping the house orderly and have no time for pleasure.
- I thought parenting would be joyful. I mean, it's meaningful, but…joy?
- I'm scared they will remember me as a raving lunatic.
- I haven't stopped to savour any moments of connection, intimacy, or emotional closeness.
- My teenagers will probably move out soon, and we have lost our connection.
- They drive me mad, and I hate their toys, but I can't imagine life without them.
- I'm the parent who I never wanted to be. I feel like it's too late to fix.

And I'm sure you could think of many more costs. When we are in doing mode, we are inadvertently teaching children that day-to-day life means getting stuff done, even at the cost of slowing down and finding joy in the present.

MEETING YOUR CHILD IN THE PRESENT MOMENT

The term mindful parenting was first coined in a 1997 book, *Everyday Blessings,* by Jon Kabat-Zinn and his wife, Myla.[15] The concept is defined as:

> Paying attention to your child and your parenting in a particular way: intentionally, here and now, and non-judgmentally, which calls to wake up to the possibilities, the benefits, and the challenges of parenting with a new awareness and intentionality, not only as if what we did mattered, but also as if our conscious engagement in parenting were virtually the most important thing we could be doing, both for our child and for ourselves.

Mindful parenting describes a type of mental state that we deliberately cultivate in the way that we pay attention to our child. Kabat-Zinn defined the three core foundations of mindful parenting as sovereignty, empathy, and acceptance. Embodying these requires addressing the recursive cycles that have been outlined across the previous three chapters. If our reactive patterns are not broken, we surpass our good intentions of granting our children a sense of sovereignty by genuinely accepting them and empathising with their experience. Sovereignty in the parent–child context means respect for their autonomy as an individual who is different from you. We don't view them as a part of who we are but rather as a whole individual, even when they are babies.

An easy way to grasp this concept is to think about how progressive schools are changing from old-school, more traditional models of the teacher being the superior and the student being more submissive to a more collaborative relationship that is grounded in mutual respect. The old-school approach would consider the student as 'just a kid' who doesn't really know what they want. Thus, adults tell them what is best for them and make important decisions without having them be heard. While parents are required to make important decisions for their children, they can do so without taking an authoritarian stance. Even if the decision is the opposite of what the child wants and the parent is required to make a hard choice, they can integrate respect for the child's autonomous experience. This includes having respectful conversations and actively listening to the child to ensure that the child's voice and opinion are heard. The child receives the message that they are worthwhile and have an important opinion, even when they do not have the ability to make the final call.

I find that for many parents, the concept of sovereignty is

disregarded as unimportant when their children are babies and toddlers. Sovereignty becomes easier to embody when their children reach the mid- to late-childhood developmental stage, before they have started to individuate from their parents. But with adolescents, it can be threatening and challenging. We will explore some examples.

I recall an uproar in Australian media about four years ago because a parenting blogger wrote on the importance of telling your child when you are going to pick them up and talking to them to explain that you're changing their nappy. It was interesting and a little alarming to see how furious many parents were. They ridiculed the blogger as an absolute joke and thought it was just absurd that they should have to 'ask consent' from a baby or toddler to change their nappy. I understood where the parents were coming from, but the essence of the message was lost. The important part was not necessarily to get 'consent' to change a nappy. It was to give the child a heads-up that they were about to be picked up and have their nappy changed. The message was grounded in granting the young child a sense of sovereignty.

I certainly don't want to increase parenting anxiety around how intense the first few years can be. However, if your children are still young babies or toddlers, sending the overarching message to them that they are respected by their parents is important. Although they won't be able to necessarily 'remember' as they get older, this is the most impressionable time when their subconscious and unconscious mind is like a sponge soaking in their environment. Their brain is wired to seek confirmation of the following questions, even before they acquire language: Am I important? Am I loveable? Am I worthy? The reason that it is easy in early- to mid-childhood is that children tend to still be under their parent's wing, and their individuation can be triggering for their parent's default, inner child, and inner parent modes.

For example, I have observed extremely loving parents laugh in their adolescent's face when they have shared their core values. '*You* have values?' their parent mocked. The parent's inner child was extremely defensive that their child's moral reasoning may reject their behaviour and started discounting it as a fallacy as quickly as possible. The parent, in this case, wanted the adolescent to change their behaviour to conform to the parent's ideals, but with the motivation of pleasing them. Not for the motivation of aligning their behaviour with their values, which was a missed opportunity for the adolescent to continue healthily developing their autonomy, positive sense of self, and individuation.

On the other hand, I have met with many parents who have worked really hard to develop self-awareness around the way they are triggered and their responses. One thing is for sure: it's not easy. Yet as we learn to look at our patterns of emotional enmeshment—where the emotional relationships within the family do not have clear personal boundaries, and the parent and child tend to absorb each other's emotions—then we can start to address the codependency that many of us have. If we are enmeshed, your emotions are my emotions. Therefore, I cannot have much empathy for your experience because I am engulfed by emotion myself.

When parents of anxious children bring them to therapy, a very effective strategy is to have them set 'worry time', which works to contain the amount of time the child gets hooked by and talks about their worries. This can help with enmeshment, too, because the parent can set some boundaries around how much they engage with the child's anxiety. Sometimes parents get quite snappy and irritated when their child shares their worries. It's not because they don't care, but usually, they are catching the child's anxiety, and their ability to support them is diminished. Bringing mindfulness to these experiences allows us to embody empathy. Empathy separates the parent's experience from the child's experience. It gives the parent permission to hold space for the child's emotion without fully absorbing it themselves.

For example, say your child comes home from school and says, 'Johnny was mean to me today. He called me an idiot.' Instead of going into ego-discrediting mode, 'Well he's an idiot', or problem-solving mode, 'What did you say back to him?', we can learn to hold space for our child's emotional experience with full acceptance and empathy. Before reacting, we learn to respond to the emotion first and foremost. 'That must have been hard. How did you feel when he said that?' Then continue to validate the emotion, 'Yeah, I can see why you would feel sad.' Unless our child is released from our patterns of enmeshment, it can be a barrier to being empathetic towards them and their experience. Both require acceptance: of who they are as individuals, and how they experience the world in a way that is separate from us. The more we practise and the more we develop mindfulness skills, the more natural it becomes.

Acceptance is simple when our child turns out exactly as we expected and meets our expectations. Yet the most important part of acceptance is how we bring it to the table when our children do not meet our expectations. How do we accept them when they are not as brilliant, smart, or sporty as we expected they would be? How do we react when they have a personality that we find difficult, or when their sexual preferences are not as we expected they would be? How do we respond to the child when they reject our religious or spiritual beliefs, or when they want something that we perceive to be wrong? To bring genuine acceptance to our children and to their experiences does not mean we have to like, embrace, and celebrate every part of them. However, we have to be willing to tolerate the discomfort so that we can embody genuine acceptance: the most important gift we can give to our children.

CHAPTER 6

Traits: Changing Your Brain

If I asked you to list the most desired traits that you hope to embody as a parent, you might say empathy, insight, compassion, calm alertness, non-reactivity, the transcendence of purely self-focussed needs, and immense internal resources and psychological resilience. These lofty aspirations coincide with the very same traits that long-term meditators have been known to cultivate.

Meditation creates short-term and long-term changes in the brain. When we cultivate a mindful state, particularly through meditation practice over time, we start to transform the function and structure of our brain, which creates altered personal traits. These traits are not something we can develop purely with good intentions. They require intention, experiential practice, structural and functional changes in the brain, and introspective experiences.

If you are new to meditation, the good news is that functional changes in the brain have been observed after just three to four *days* of practice at retreats. If you have an irregular practice, this chapter will inspire you to prioritise your practice to continue to reap the cumulative benefits. Finally, if you consider yourself a committed long-term meditator, we will explore some of the anti-aging and superhuman benefits that some relatively new research has shown.

One of the very important and life-changing benefits for parents, after even a relatively short period of practice, is how it improves their sleep. From the sleep deprivation that having babies and young children brings to insomnia—which is an ongoing issue for exhausted parents, even when their children are sleeping through the night. Many are unaware that the state of their nervous system is what contributes to poor sleep, and meditating daily could make an immense improvement. For example, a 2019 meta-analysis and systematic review evaluated eighteen studies with 1,654 participants who experienced disturbed sleep patterns. They found that mindfulness meditation, usually practised for ten to twenty minutes twice a day, was effective in addressing sleep disturbances, such as insomnia.[16] In fact, there is a whole body of research indicating how meditation causes deep rest for the brain, assisting when we have not had enough sleep, as well as promoting a better quality of sleep. Improved sleep is an important aspect of addressing stress cycles for parents and begins developing the freedom of choice in their responses. Let me explain.

Imagine that you live a ten-minute walk from the beach. To get there, you walk through the bushland. Because you take the same route each day, you have created a walking track through the bushland. You don't even need to think or plan in order to find your way. You could take a different route, but you don't see a problem with the old route. It gets you to where you want to go. But one day, you decide to go a different way. You notice you feel a little more anxious than usual. When you start to feel lost, you just jump straight back on your old route.

This analogy is similar to how our brain and neural pathways work. We naturally follow the paths that are indented, stronger, and wired together. Familiarity makes us feel safe and secure, even if we are going the long way. Even if we don't know of the fruits and flowers we could walk past on another route. Even if we don't know about a waterfall and natural rocks that we could find on another route to the same destination. We are probably more likely to go in the new direction if someone tells us about it, as it feels less risky, and also there is a promising reward that we now know about. But would we wander to find it ourselves? Often, we wouldn't. When our brains are wired for default mode, even if we have the intention to react differently by taking a new path, we tend to fall back into the crevasses of the old path—reinforcing our habitual autopilot responses.

Here's the thing: until you experience a new path, you wouldn't have the hindsight to realise the depth of the former crevasses. They were so familiar that you were blind to them. You now have the freedom to decide which way you are going. The freedom of choice is maintained by regular meditation practice, and it smooths out new crevasses in the pathways as they arise. Neurons that fire together, wire together. Everything else gets pruned as we are not using it. Thus, the crevasses reflect the wiring of our brain. We can't just change it with intention alone; we must practise taking different paths, so we forge new neural pathways and circuits.

I want you to imagine that meditation changes your brain in the following way: every time you meditate for twenty minutes, the crevasses in your familiar paths start to become less prominent. If you meditate daily, you have more chances of clearing your old paths. So, when you walk to the beach, you can go any way you like with a sense of wonder. Instead of walking a predetermined path that was shaped by an old version of yourself, influenced by your environment, your family, your friends, your culture, and your conditioning at large, you get to decide if you want to walk on a new path.

As mothers start to sleep better and deactivate their default mode pathways, the brain-body changes continue to create a ripple effect. Creating space for a new path helps to release old stress patterns, which translates to how we connect with our children. Starting from pregnancy, maternal stress can have a measurable impact on the child's temperament from infancy to childhood. It is ideal for growing babies to not be exposed to chronic stress and the cocktail of hormones, including cortisol, that is secreted in the stressed state. However, I do not subscribe to the rabbit hole of 'the damage is done, and it's all my fault'. I do not wish to put any additional pressure onto the shoulders of parents—women especially—and tend to shy away from discussing topics that could be internalised as a mother blaming herself for her child's difficulties.

There are always ways that we can help our child regardless of how many times we have made mistakes or internalised shame from the past. When a parent comes to me with an explanation as to why their adolescent is going off the rails—usually referencing something from pregnancy or infancy—it's quite often irrelevant to the here and now. We might acknowledge it and then come back to how to repair the connection, how to set boundaries, and how to create a safe base at home for them.

The pressure to not feel stressed while parenting can be a source of stress itself, which is where meditation comes in. There is a growing body of research that shows how effective meditation practice is for promoting well-being in prenatal mothers. As we only know of the adverse effects of chronic psychological distress during pregnancy, we cannot measure the full extent of the positive effects of how meditation impacts the baby and their temperament into childhood. However, there is sufficient research to assume that it is a positive, preventative practice.

For example, mothers who have participated in mindfulness intervention during pregnancy have shown to have an improved sense of maternal–fetal attachment and connection before birth.[17] Even at six months postpartum, mindful traits predicted the mother's ability to respond to infant distress, indicating greater attunement to their baby.[18] Mindful traits were broken down into two aspects: acting with awareness and describing the baby's experience. Study after study shows how mindful parenting continues to improve parent–child connection, interaction, and attachment, even when parenting teenagers.

How could this be effective at every chronological age and developmental stage? I think the simple answer is this: meditation practice changes the parent's brain, which inherently enhances areas that have to do with empathy, insight, compassion, and prosocial behaviours.[19] It strengthens the parts of the brain that are associated with picking up on emotional cues, the mental states of others, and more subtle emotional experiences making us better able to respond earlier. We become naturally less fixated on behavioural control and embody a wider sense of awareness to the whole being of our child.

MEDITATION CHANGES THE STRUCTURE AND FUNCTION OF THE BRAIN

A structural change is a visible difference that can be detected by viewing a before-and-after image of the brain, whereas a functional change occurs when the neural pathways of the brain have altered. A functional change usually means the way different regions of the brain communicate has changed, which can alter the processing of information. When we identify a structural change, this is likely associated with a functional change as well. Thus, if the brain looks different or healthier, it is functioning in a healthier way too.

Neuroscientific studies use a range of neuroimaging tools to measure how meditation practice changes the brain. For example, magnetic resonance imaging (MRI) takes a photo-like image to display structural changes. A more dynamic tool, such as *functional* magnetic resonance imaging (fMRI; measures changes associated with blood flow) or an electroencephalogram (EEG; measures brain waves), measures a change in brain function. Advancements in neuroscientific research have taught us a great deal about how meditation changes our brain. Given the brain is an incredibly complex organ in humans, we are only going to scrape the surface of the neuroscience that underlies these processes.

As we age, it is developmentally expected that the brain shrinks in size, white matter, and grey matter, which is associated with cognitive decline. Neuroscientists have shown that in the brains of long-term meditators, their brain mass size appears to be approximately seven years younger than the same-aged brains of non-meditators. A 2005 study conducted by a Massachusetts neuroscience research team compared brain scans of experienced insight meditators who incorporated daily meditation into their family, social, and professional lives with the scans of non-meditators. They found that the cortical thickness of forty- to fifty-year-old meditators was comparable to the brain scans of non-meditators aged twenty to thirty years old.[20] Consistent with other studies, meditation appears to slow age-related thinning of the prefrontal cortex (located behind your forehead) with increased volume of grey matter in areas that involve attention and sensory awareness.[21] While these are exciting long-term changes, even after a brief three-day meditation retreat, the amygdala (trigger of the stress response) shrinks in size and the prefrontal cortex thickens.[22]

In terms of structural changes, it can be helpful to think of it like this: we want parts of the brain associated with psychological stress to shrink in size while parts of the brain associated with well-being increase in size. The bigger in size, the more strength and power a part of the brain has over our default responses, making us more likely to fall into the crevasses of old and unhelpful or new and helpful pathways. An example of a brain region that is ideal to develop in creating superior pathways is the thickening of grey matter density in the prefrontal cortex. This region above our eyebrows has an essential role that governs the way we react and respond in daily life, known as *executive functioning*. Our executive function determines our attentional bias—what cues we focus on, how impulsive we are, or how we self-regulate and inhibit our reactions. It is essential in decision-making, problem-solving, self-control, moderating social behaviour, making decisions based on long-term goals, and ultimately the quality to act with self-awareness and emotional intelligence. For every parent discussed in each unique case study, strengthening their prefrontal cortex would be helpful in making positive parenting changes in their everyday life.

As well as increased grey matter, meditation creates more white matter in the brain. White matter is a vast interconnected system of neural connections that acts as a connector of the lobes of the brain. It connects the complex maps between the limbic (emotional) system and the prefrontal cortex (executive function) systems. Why is this important? The white matter tract—known as the corpus collosum located in the midline of the brain—is strengthened to bridge the right and left hemispheres. When the right and left hemispheres of the brain communicate more clearly, we have a more coherent brain. This is a key reason why meditators feel 'smarter' or actually become smarter (reflected by higher IQ scores) than before they meditated: because the hemispheres are working in unison, and communication channels are more fluid and clearer. The by-product can be clarity of thought and improved mood. It also explains why meditators tend to perform better under pressure or stress and tend to show improved academic, occupational, and test performance.

Peer-reviewed research and personal anecdotes also report that meditation appears to increase innovation, creativity, and 'creative intelligence', which is likely the result of improved neural coherence between the right and left hemispheres as well. The performance-based benefits are really an external reflection of what is happening internally. As the default mode network is deactivated, we develop greater introspective reflection with the ability to hold a sense of mindful presence. This allows us to get in touch with a part of the mind that transcends our ruminative thought patterns and is overly involved with self-referencing 'me' thinking and getting stuck by our cognitive patterns.

In Western psychology, we tend to accept three states of consciousness: sleep, dream, and wakefulness. In a sense, meditation cultivates a different state of consciousness, often described as a state of calm-and-alert awareness or wakefulness. Eastern philosophy and modern mysticism refer to this as the 'fourth state of consciousness' synonymously referred to as transcendence. In spiritual circles, transcendence is the idea that we can experience an altered state of consciousness outside of the field that we experience in material life, with a sense of connectedness to other people, nature, and to a form of mystical connection to something greater than ourselves.

When it comes to meditation, the closest that scientists come to measuring this proposed 'fourth state' of consciousness is through EEG studies that show altered brain waves that tend to vary slightly depending on which type of meditation is practised. Although modern psychology is not concerned with an individual's religious or spiritual beliefs, we do know that having a sense of connectedness to something that is greater than oneself is a positive 'protective' factor for our well-being. It is something that tends to help us humans get through inevitable difficult times, especially when facing some of life's biggest challenges—loneliness, illness, disability, death, grief, and loss. It's also useful when navigating our collective sense of lack of purpose and addiction to external things—validation, busyness, and material possessions.

Neural trait changes encourage positive parenting by making us better able to attend to what is most important without feeling inundated by everyday responsibilities. For example, instead of mindlessly fixating on daily chores, the parent can bring heightened awareness to their patterns of behaviour and more flexibly respond to their child—even when the dishes need to be done. This combination of presence and flexibility is different from multitasking, or attention-splitting, which is not good for our brain and psychological well-being.

Parents, particularly new parents, have periods of sleep deprivation and physical caregiving demands that exceed their supply of internal resources. Not only do the functional changes in the brain and nervous system reduce psychological symptoms (improved sleep, mood, recovery from stressors) and physiological stress (heart rate variability, blood pressure, cortisol levels, etc.), but they also impact the immune system and the expression of gene activity.

MEDITATION HAS AN EPIGENETIC EFFECT

Epigenetics is the study of how our DNA genes change and regulate, why some are activated, and why others are not without modification of the gene sequence. It helps us to understand how our genes adapt based on environmental and lifestyle factors. For example, a 2014 study led by Richard Davidson found an 'epigenetic effect'—a lower expression of genes involved in inflammation and molecules that activate genes—in experienced meditators compared to control conditions.[23] In other words, those who meditate were at lower risk of switching on particular genes, so to speak, that trigger inflammation and other physical health problems that are highly associated with disease and illness. The researchers concluded that this epigenetic effect on the de-regulation of genes reflected the therapeutic potential of mindfulness-based interventions, not just in mental healthcare but in healthcare overall. Such findings also show that meditation is an extremely helpful practice to prevent the onset of poor well-being—both physically and psychologically.

Chronic stress is a huge risk factor for developing chronic illness, so it makes good sense that mindfulness meditation practice can improve physical health too, especially as a *preventative* measure. In a 2016 systematic review of twenty randomised, controlled trials comprising more than 1,600 participants, researchers found that mindfulness meditation was associated with positive changes in select immune system processes involved in inflammation, immunity, and biological aging.[24] They focussed on five different biomarkers of immunity, including circulating and stimulated inflammatory proteins, cellular transcription factors and gene expression, immune cell count, immune cell aging, and antibody response. We have all had the experience of being run down and knowing that we are coming down with a cold or flu—due to our compromised immune system.

Although we may be 'predisposed' to particular psychological and physical illnesses, our genetics are not our destiny. Changes in short-term states of our body can lead to long-term health improvements, even when we are susceptible to certain particular psychological or physical conditions due to hereditary factors and family history. Our lifestyle plays a very important role in our health and well-being. A regular meditation practice can replenish the depletion of our mind, body, and spirit from the inside out.

YOU DON'T HAVE TO BE A MONK TO MEDITATE

When researchers studied the brains of monks who had between 12,000 and 62,000 hours of practice experience, they found near-superhuman traits.[25] If becoming a monk is not something that you're interested in, that is absolutely fine. Remember, the brain can show functional changes after just three days of consistent practice. If you decide on twenty minutes per day, you're still going to reap some incredible benefits for your mental health and well-being.

As a psychologist, I know that we humans are much more likely to stick to things when we are reinforced. Thus, there must be a sense of intrinsic reinforcement for people to choose to spend the first waking moments of their day sitting on their meditation mat, day in, day out, for forty years. The incredible impact of long-term meditation is also a little nudge of encouragement for those who, like me, feel inspired to stay committed. I gain inspiration from people who have been meditating every day for decades. They will tell you that it is the gift that keeps giving and that they continue to feel cumulative benefits from their practice.

While we are losing something, we also must be gaining something. This combination is powerful in reinforcing us to show up and come back to the mat when we have fallen out of the habit. This research describes a change in the brain that may be an answer to what keeps us going after so many years. Richard Davidson, one of the most influential meditation neuroscience researchers in the world studied the brains of twenty-one Olympian meditators to see if their heightened states experienced during meditation paired with the practice of present-moment attention, openness, and non-judgement transferred to become new personality traits that could be observed in their brain patterns.[26] Most of the research on individuals new to meditation demonstrates changes in the alpha, theta, beta, and delta waves. However, in long-term seasoned meditators, the research shows incredible coherent patterns of gamma waves rhythmically flowing ('oscillating', according to neuroscientists) in synchrony across the whole brain that were *lasting*. Most of us may show gamma waves from time to time and short bursts, usually for a fifth of a second—in a fleeting moment of bliss. High, lasting gamma waves are something entirely unique to long-term meditators.

The most interesting finding was observed when scanning and measuring the brain of the now world-renowned Tibetan Buddhist Master, Yongey Mingyur Rinpoche.[27] He had more than 62,000 hours of meditation practice, including ten full years of retreat—possibly the most experienced meditator in the world. When his brain was scanned recently when he was forty-one years old, neuroscientists reported that his brain resembled that of a thirty-three-year-old. The research team had initially thought that the EEG machine measuring this monk's brain was faulty or broken as the results seemed to defy all scientific logic.[28] They were witnessing a 'critical inflection point in neuroscience history'—levels of gamma waves in the human brain that had simply never been observed before. His gamma waves peaked 700 to 800 percent in a few seconds during meditation, bursting for minutes instead of split seconds. This was thought to represent a special state of consciousness that most of us have not obtained.

When Mingyur Rinpoche shifted from a meditative state—meditating on loving-kindness and compassion—

to a resting state, unusually high gamma waves were still visible and measurable. Based on the extraordinary synchronised brain patterns observed, Mingyur Rinpoche has since been labelled the 'happiest man in the world'. This has not occurred through positive thinking but from his extraordinary awareness and long-term meditation practice. The level of alertness combined with profound relaxation is the unique result of regular and committed practice.

Although there are different forms of meditation that appear to yield slightly different results, they all contribute to some shared benefits. For example, a 2018 study led by neurosurgeons measured the effects of the four main types of meditation: focussed attention, open-monitoring, transcendental, and loving-kindness meditation.[29] All four types were associated with a slight difference in local changes in different regions of the brain. However, increased frequency of high gamma waves in the frontal region was consistently observed compared to non-meditators with greater effects associated with longer-term practice. Similarly, all styles of meditation have been associated with enhanced alpha wave activity during and after meditation, which is why we feel a calm and relaxed alertness during and after meditating, and why long-term meditators report feeling at ease overall compared to novices.

While my personal preference is transcendental meditation, the key is to find a meditation that you enjoy, that works for you, and that you're actually going to practise. If it's 'working for you', meaning that you are internally reinforced because you are *experiencing* benefits, you will more likely remain committed.

CHAPTER 7

Presence: Cultivating Mindful States

One of the reasons that I enjoy writing in the morning is because I can shift into full presence. This, in essence, is the practice of deactivating my default mode and diminishing the ego. In the moments of 'writer's block', there is more mental chatter, self-doubt, defensiveness, and editing as I go, instead of just writing and creating. Writer's block, or any mental block, means that we are hooked or fusing with our thoughts. The ego is back in action. By learning to cultivate a mindful state, we experience a sense of flow. The flow state was coined and popularised by psychologist Mihaly Csíkszentmihályi.[30] It describes a mindful state where we are fully immersed in an activity with a sense of total awareness, focus, and enjoyment in the process. In this state, we tend to experience a calm alertness. We may become completely absorbed and lose track of time.

Cultivating mindfulness requires us to deactivate the default mode network to fully pay attention to the present moment. We can experience a flow state by engaging in a task, activity, or movement. Some common examples are sport, cooking, music, art, performing, writing, being in the forest, gardening, and so on. The intention is not to try to bring about a particular emotion or experience but rather to be fully present and immersed, generating positive emotions like curiosity and joy as a by-product. In his 2004 TED Talk, Csíkszentmihályi suggested, 'There's this focus that, once it becomes intense, leads to a sense of ecstasy, a sense of clarity: you know exactly what you want to do from one moment to the other; you get immediate feedback.'[31] The feedback is intrinsic. With his research team, Csíkszentmihályi identified six factors as encompassing an experience of a flow state:

1. Intense and focused concentration on the present moment.
2. Merging of action and awareness.
3. A loss of reflective self-consciousness.
4. A sense of personal control or agency over the situation or activity.
5. A distortion of temporal experience; one's subjective experience of time is altered.

6. Experience of the activity as intrinsically rewarding; an autotelic experience.

Mindfulness is not about controlling an experience but rather being open to whatever experience is arising in the present. We often think of these states as grandiose events that only exceptional people can cultivate—artists, authors, athletes. It is actually through the most mundane moments that we can practise finding bliss in the present, when doing chores or repetitive tasks that come with raising children.

Starting in the morning, we can create total immersions around an everyday task that helps us shift from stressed to mindful states. For example, let's say that you wake up to an infant or toddler, and the first thing that you need to do is say good morning and change their nappy. You may create a process of total immersion from first glance. You make eye contact and really notice the colour of your child's eyes. Notice how they seem to be feeling by observing their body language and facial expressions. It doesn't matter what emotions, mood, or behaviour they seem to be displaying. There is no preference. Just focus on the full awareness of what you're observing. As you pick them up, notice the feel of their skin and how warm or cool they feel. As you change the nappy, bring your attention to the child so intently, as if it is the only time you will see them all day. There is an abundance of experiences we can immerse ourselves in during moments like these.

If your children are at school and the first thing that you do in the morning is get up and start making lunches or preparing breakfast for the family, you can use that task as your mindful morning immersion. You can pay attention to the light, the warmth, and the feel of your feet on the kitchen floor. The smells, colours, and textures of the food. Many people choose to use cooking as a way to practise mindful immersion. Given it's a necessary self-care task, it can be an excellent way to create an early evening immersion as well.

You can create your experience with music on, focus on the repetition of cutting, and notice the texture and the way that preparing, cooking, and eating food engages all of your senses in different ways. It does not have to be a fancy meal that takes more than ten minutes to prepare. It's just about setting the intention and bringing your full attention to one task.

BREATHING OUR WAY BACK

To become more holistically mindful in our lives, it starts with how we relate to our body and breath. We need to develop self-awareness that, at all times, we are influencing the nervous system to do one of three things:

1. To accumulate stress by contributing to the stress response.
2. To maintain an already sympathetic-dominant stressed state.
3. To recover and rebalance stressors to remain in a homeostatic state.

Working with the breath is one of the most effective ways that we can move with our nervous system to recover from stress and rebalance ourselves.[32] Not only can our breath be used as a focal point to direct our attention, but it is also the most effective way to shift our stress response. By breathing, we alert the parasympathetic nervous system to recover from the stress response, which helps to bring our brain, body, and senses back to a homeostatic state. Working with the breath is an effective way to learn how to develop the ability to respond instead of to react.

In relation to parenting, we can use the breath as a tool to self-regulate in order to respond instead of reacting to our reaction. This involves a process of having space within our window of tolerance to breathe through the peak of the response. We can improve how quickly we are able to recover from the stressor in order to respond from a balanced state. When we notice a minor trigger, we can pause and take seven deep, slow, and controlled breaths to help us move through the peak of our trigger. In other situations, we may need to remove ourselves for a few minutes to sit down and create a breathing space.

Taking a deep and controlled breath is a shortcut to stimulate the vagus nerve, which stimulates the parasympathetic nervous system. The physiology of the nervous system then works with your mind to rebalance and come back to being present and responsive. You can think of the vagus nerve as a dictator of the parasympathetic nervous system, just as the amygdala unconsciously dictates the sympathetic stress response. This is why when we pause to take slow, deep, and controlled breaths when we are triggered, we can rebalance in order to respond effectively.

When the vagal tone is high, our body relaxes and recovers faster after stress. Slow and deep-controlled breathing from the diaphragm is known to increase the tone of the vagus nerve, making our nervous system more responsive and tolerant. The scientific research of breathwork and breathing practices is rapidly growing in complexity. When we practise deep and slow controlled breathing, our physiological improvements tend to be connected to our psychological well-being.

For Sarah from the first chapter, starting a mindful breathing practice was her first step towards changing her stress patterns. Mindful breathing helped her to work with the natural regulation mechanisms of her nervous system throughout the day, especially when getting her son ready for school. She integrated a three-minute breathing space in the morning and in the afternoon, which later became a regular part of her mindfulness practice. Sarah also reported that her husband started his own breathing practice as she modelled the improvements it was bringing to her daily life.

Integrating more regular work with the breath is extremely useful for parents as it can be a preventative practice to stay in balance and a reactive strategy to restore balance. Breathing functions as a brief but powerful intervention to circuit break in the midst of a struggle. We can set intentions to engage in daily formal breath meditation, but most importantly, at any time of day, regardless of what is going on around us, we can remember to breathe.

As you read this sentence, bring your attention to your breath. Notice how it is working with or without your conscious effort. Notice the natural rhythm of your breath. Is it shallow? Are you breathing to your chest? As you have been paying attention to it for a few seconds now, you may have already noticed a change in the rhythm.

Anytime when you want to engage in a brief mindful breathing practice, follow these three simple steps:

1. First, bring narrowly focussed attention to your

thoughts, feelings, and sensations in the here and now. You can notice and label your experience by making a mental note. For example, 'judging', 'ruminating', or 'angry'.
2. Second, shift your attention and focus on the breath as it moves in and out of your nose and mouth, slowly and deeply, for at least one minute. The higher your peak reaction means the more minutes you can focus on your breath.
3. Third, expand your attention to create a wider field of awareness around your breath, body, and surroundings in the environment. Bring this sense of expanded awareness and connection to the breath with you as you go on with your day.

For parents, bringing more intentional breathwork and breath connection into their daily lives can help to break the automatic reactions that occur from all cycles: survival mode, schema modes, ego reactions, or default mode. By starting with slow breathing, we can practise landing in the present.

MINDFUL MOVEMENT

The breath and body are often referred to as the anchor to the present. This is because at any given moment, our breath and body are present even when our mind is elsewhere: in the past, future, at work, or in our stream of constant ruminations. Mindfulness is a way to bring our wandering mind and attention back to the body.

During periods of time when I have taken on too much—too many work hours, rushing around, too much time in counselling where I often have bad posture, and too many hours hunched over at my computer screen—I feel less connected to my body, which is a sign of being less present. My body communicates with me when I am falling out of balance. It starts with subtle headaches and minor neck or back pain. If I don't tune in and listen to these signs, it ends in more severe headaches and intense back and neck pain that require pain relief. Years ago, I had to reach full-blown depletion before I would pay attention. These days, I live with a greater connection to my body, which for me, is also a sign of self-respect.

There are many different ways that we can become more attuned to our body, from a mindfulness body scan practice to mindful movements, such as mindful walking, stretching, or a more formal practice like yoga. A walking meditation, or walking with awareness, is a great way to start practising mindful states if you feel resistant to sitting down for formal meditation. When we go for a walk, we often do something else, like listen to a podcast or make a phone call. However, for the purposes of reconnecting with the body, a walking meditation involves engaging in no distractions. As we can walk on autopilot, at first, our mind will likely start wandering immediately. We might even notice the mind resisting being 'bored' and feeling emotionally irritable. Especially if you have just started a mindful walking practice, you need to make space for these feelings as you simply unhook from them and bring your attention back to awareness.

The practice of walking with awareness means that we pay attention to the way the body feels as we walk, the sway and sensation of the movement, and the rhythm of our feet as we step left, then right, and follow the feeling of our feet on the ground. With attention to what is going on around you, you notice the sounds, the smells, and the sights. Although walking in a beautiful forest can be particularly pleasant, we can actually practise mindful walking in any urban environment.

The quality of the practice is dependent upon the quality of attention to our experience in the present. Regardless of what is in your surroundings, you can tune in to what is happening around you—from other people walking by, birds chirping, cars passing, beeping, city sounds, the sound of a train passing by, trees swaying, or waves crashing—or anything else that arises in your awareness. The idea is to unhook from judgements, 'the sunset was better yesterday' or 'the winds are cold', to notice what you see here and now. Each time the mind has wandered, you can simply and gently bring it back to the body. Such a practice can be as short as ten minutes around a city block.

Some people love hiking for hours. Some mindfully run. For my husband, surfing cultivates his mindful states. Others turn to yoga, which, like mindful walking, incorporates the body, the breath, and the mind in the present. There is a significant body of research that justifies integrating a mindful-movement routine as part of stress and well-being management. In 2017, a meta-analysis reviewed the findings of forty-two studies measuring the physiological effects of yoga.[33] Results revealed that yoga asanas (basic positions) were associated with reduced cortisol levels in the evening and in the morning. They also found improvements in blood pressure, resting heart rate, and heart rate variability. The authors concluded that the mindful practice of yoga asanas was overall associated with improved regulation of the sympathetic nervous system and the adrenal system across various populations.

Many parents—fathers especially—have a resistance to yoga because of the way the wellness industry has marketed it as a feminine practice. Notice what comes to mind when I invite you to imagine someone who does yoga daily. Did you imagine a beautiful young woman in a tight-fitting outfit doing an intimidating pose? But yoga does not require a certain body type, flexibility, or outfit. In essence, yoga combines guided slow and controlled breathing exercises, focussing of the mind, and deep relaxation in the body.

Sometimes people come to yoga to improve their performance in another sport, but they report it is not a good 'workout' itself. Usually, in response to this, we need to come back to psycho-physiological education: yoga is a restoring, rebalancing, and recovery practice with the added benefit of improving flexibility and strength. Many people who live in fight-flight gravitate towards more intense physical activity, which has many health benefits. However, high-intensity exercise can be another source of physiological stress, which is why our well-being benefits when we integrate mindfulness practices to help work with the autonomic nervous system to repair the accumulation of stress.

When beginners feel irritable or bored in yoga, it is because they are struggling to be truly present. This discomfort is part of the process. Finding ease in awareness takes practice. But mindful movement does not have to be complicated; it can be as simple as fifteen minutes of breathing, body poses, and reconnecting with the body before climbing into bed. As we incorporate these practices into our daily lives, we develop more internal resources and strength in our nervous system to break our own stress cycles and respond more effectively to our children.

We all do things every single day that we could use for mindful awareness immersion. The key is not in the activity that we choose; it is the way in which we practise it—the intention behind our attention.

CHAPTER 8

Meditate: A Committed Practice

Formal meditation practice is, in essence, attention training. It is a practice that involves sharpening the psychological tool of paying attention. Most of us spend half our lives distracted, mind wandering, and essentially, in default mode. That means, we probably spend at least half of our time with our children in this very same distracted state. Unless we actively train our attention, there is usually a disparity between our good intentions and alignment of conscious choices, which includes our parenting behaviours.

We don't meditate to get better at meditation; we meditate to get better at life. To decide if we want to set the intention to meditate, we should not measure it based on how well we can currently concentrate or focus our attention. We should measure it based on how satisfied, calm, connected, compassionate, and meaningful our life feels. For parents, we can measure our meditation practice based on how we are showing up with our children. The key to starting and committing to a new meditation practice is when the costs of not learning outweigh the discomfort of beginning a new skill.

My meditation teacher once said to me that when you meditate, you make better decisions. Of course, neuroscience supports this as the prefrontal cortex functions better, and we activate more introspective and reflective parts of the self that can align with our values and long-term desires. However, there is a more mysterious aspect too, one that can't be fully captured by words. The way in which I make decisions has changed, and the decisions I have made since learning to meditate have changed my life in ways that I could never have imagined. Where we focus our attention and the decisions that we make determine our life. Only with conscious attention and awareness comes personal freedom and liberation.

OVERCOMING THE BARRIERS

If you're reading this, we can assume that you can relate to one of two experiences. You have a committed meditation practice, and you continue to meditate because of the cumulative benefits, which internally reinforces you. Or, you are with the majority and have had some brief meditation experience that did not become a long-term practice. To overcome our barriers, it's important to acknowledge what they are and how they hold us back. Most people come with a pre-existing attitude towards meditation that tends to include the three main stories acting as mental barriers to starting and committing to a meditation practice:

- The 'I can't stop my thoughts and clear my mind' or 'I get too distracted and can't concentrate' story.
- The 'I don't have time' or 'I'm too busy' story.
- The 'I've tried, and it doesn't work for me' story.

Meditation is probably one of the only skills that we do once or twice and expect to achieve Olympic-level results. If you're a beginner, you're not supposed to be able to sit down, clear your mind, transcend, and experience profound relaxation and gamma waves. You're not supposed to experience anything other than what you experience. This would be like going to your first-ever basketball game, with no training, and expect to play like Michael Jordan. And when we inevitably perceive failure, we decide that the activity is not for us because we don't have one of those 'special' kinds of brains. Those special brains are simply cultivated through practice—showing up to the mat, time and time again, without expectations of sustained perpetual bliss.

Thoughts are a natural part of meditation just as weeds are a natural part of a garden. They are just following the default crevasses in our brain that have been reinforced over many years. We do not have to pull out the weeds or get rid of thoughts at all. The key to any meditation practice is effortlessness. The practice will naturally dissolve the weeds and reform the crevasses with consistent practice over time. How we react to thoughts during meditation is more important than if we have thoughts or none at all. Trying to clear your mind will just lead to resistance and frustration. Regardless of your meditation technique, simply allow your thoughts to come and go without getting caught up and reacting to them.

Even when we have been meditating for many years, the essence of the practice itself involves non-striving and effortlessness. It is not another means for us to strive for perfectionism or continual improvement. All meditation teachers will tell you that there is no such thing as a 'good' or 'bad' meditation. Sometimes you may experience moments or extended moments of perpetual bliss, and other times you may experience uncomfortable emotions. We can simply bring curiosity and openness to painful emotions and allow them to come and go naturally. This is a natural part of the self-regulation process.

BRIEF PRIMING PRACTICE

When starting meditation, it can be helpful to practise a brief five- to ten-minute practice each morning to help prime the mind for meditation. You are welcome to read the following passage and self-guide your practice or download an audio-guided priming practice from www.reneecachia.com. The intention of this practice is to just simply notice when the mind wanders and when you are able to bring your attention back. Then you are practising mindfulness meditation.

> Find a comfortable place to sit on a seat or on a cushion on the floor so that the bottom half of your body forms a stable base, with your back sitting straight against a wall or chair. Allow your shoulders to relax fully. Place your hands on your knees or in a comfortable position resting on your lap. When you feel ready, allow your eyes to close or gently gaze towards the floor.
>
> Set the intention for the practice to simply notice when your mind wanders and to gently bring your attention back with an attitude of kindness and curiosity.
>
> Take a moment to notice how the chair or ground holds your body. Notice the points of contact between your body and the seat, cushion, or floor. If you are sitting, you might notice the sensation of the floor beneath your feet, the chair against your legs, and your lower back against the

chair. Bring awareness to the wholeness of your body in the moment.

Noticing each in-breath and out-breath, pay attention to the sensation and rhythm of your breathing without trying to change or regulate it. As you sit, continue to rest your attention on the sensation of the breath moving in through your nose, expanding your lungs, and then moving out through your mouth as your chest deflates.

Each time you notice your mind wandering, just acknowledge that you have noticed your attention drifting away, which means you have come back to the practice. Your mind is doing exactly what it is made to do. Priming your mind for meditation is simply the practice of gently bringing the attention back to the focal point—the breath.

Now gently bring your attention back to your body, noticing your posture, the points of contact with the chair or floor, and allow your attention to explore any physical sensations that arise. Notice any sounds in the room or outside of the room you are in as you start to prepare to open your eyes and bring this sense of awareness back to the rest of your day.

A PRACTICE TO TRANSFORM PARENTING

When Sarah was first introduced to a meditation practice, she reported all of the most common challenges that were holding back her ongoing practice: a lack of time, a busy mind, and an internal struggle with her own willingness and deservingness to carve out the time for herself. She figured that, given she was not doing a great job at parenting—the most important part of her life—she did not deserve to take ten to fifteen minutes out of her day to nourish her own inner resources. Despite her perception that she was selfish to take this time out for herself, it was actually the least selfish thing that she could do. The nervous system of her family relied on the robustness of her nervous system. She started to learn that her children's emotional difficulties were being fed by her reactiveness, and their well-being was nourished by her responsiveness.

As Sarah started to articulate the costs and benefits of making a change, she was able to face her resistance to meditation. To do so, she needed to get very clear on *why* she wanted to make this change. She needed to set her intentions. These would serve as her own reminder, when she was experiencing a million competing demands, why her practice was her priority. There were layers to Sarah's intentions, from starting to shift her state out of constant survival and default mode to developing a stronger spiritual connection and sense of connectedness in the world. To gain clarity, she wrote down her intentions with a rationale to clearly define why she wanted to commit to a new practice when she knew resistance would arise at some point. This process also shed light on her core values.

INTENTION: TO IMPROVE MY WELL-BEING OVERALL

- To shift from a constant state of stress to a state of balance and well-being.
- To better manage my stress for the sake of my physical health and well-being, which may support a healthier heart rate, blood pressure, and reduce my somatic symptoms.

INTENTION: TO BECOME THE PARENT I WANT TO BE

- To learn to respond to my children in a calmer and more patient way without flying off the handle.
- To become better at paying attention to emotions in the family, noticing my own emotional states, and recognising the changing emotional states of my children without feeling responsible for changing or fixing them.
- To start to model a healthier response to and relationship with stress for my children so that they can learn how to manage their emotions in a healthy way.
- To deepen my emotional connection with my children to strengthen our relationship, especially as they are getting older by the day.

INTENTION: TO CULTIVATE VITALITY, CONNECTION, AND MEANING IN LIFE

- To develop clarity of thought and a sense of clear-

mindedness after years of anxiety, rumination, and worry.
- To support my personal reflection of my life to empower me to make supportive decisions for my life circumstances.
- To have the openness to develop a connection to myself and a spiritual connection to the world—connections that I have always struggled to secure.
- To commit to a personal practice that helps me be more present and to experience a sense of meaning in my everyday life.

Once Sarah had broken down her personal barriers and clarified her intentions, the third and essential step to success was to create a new daily habit and to form clear and consistent boundaries around her practice. Whilst adopting an attitude of self-kindness, curiosity, and flexibility to meditation is important, when developing a new practice and skill, supportive habits and boundaries are what forms discipline and commitment. Over time, a practice becomes more flexible and can be done in different ways, places, and with different schedules. However, to get started, Sarah's success plan looked like this:

- When: At 6:00–6:15 a.m., I will move to the floor to meditate. I will meditate in my car after work between 4:00–4:15 p.m.
- Where: I will meditate in the morning sitting on the

floor beside my bed and sitting in the car before I leave work in the afternoon.
- How: I will start by using guided meditations that I have downloaded in advance.
- Supportive behaviours: Going to bed by 10:00 p.m., disabling social media apps from my phone for a period of time, moving my phone away from the bed, and leaving work on time.
- Personal boundaries: I commit to meditating for at least ten minutes before leaving my bedroom in the morning. If I miss my afternoon meditation, I will protect at least ten minutes to meditate before I go to bed that night.
- Skill development: I will enrol in a meditation training course or weekly class to support me to further develop my practice and to remain accountable.

Of course, many parents would say, 'but I have three young children… I don't get a break at all!' While this life stage may require more flexibility than when children are less dependent, it also means much stronger personal boundaries are required around self-care. Depending on each unique situation, there will be different barriers and resources that we can lean on to create space for self-care. This might include seeking support from a co-parent to help you protect this time and practice, using naptimes to meditate, teaching young children to create quiet time using a timer, accepting external help that is available, and so on. It is rarely easy, but it is a necessity.

DEVELOPING MEDITATION TECHNIQUES

A common misconception that we have is that meditation is a blanket word for one type of practice that involves sitting still and clearing the mind. This is like assuming that there is only one kind of sport. If you have tried or toyed with one meditation technique and assume that you can't meditate, don't give up. It's like Michael Jordan trying tennis for the first time and concluding that sport is not for him, or if Tiger Woods lost in a race to Usain Bolt and decided that he should not bother with sport anymore. These examples seem silly because we know that there are many different forms of sport, and these different professional and Olympic-level athletes cannot be fairly compared across their different areas of expertise. However, when Michael Jordan tried his hand at baseball or golf, he could train to a higher level than someone who was not already an elite athlete. Meditation is similar; if we have accumulated our hours of practice in one style of meditation, it's going to be much easier to drop in to try or start another style of practice. First, because our brain has changed to support this, and second, because we have transferrable meditative skills.

While there are thousands of research studies that dive into the intricacies of the overlapping and unique benefits of each different type of distinct meditation practice, there is no superior practice. The practice for you is the one that you are able and willing to commit to on a regular and consistent basis, because that practice will be more effective than any other form of inconsistent practice. The perfect amount of time to practise is for as long as it is sustainable for you, as the benefits are cumulative. The more you practise, the stronger the benefits you will reap. Consider it your unique personal training program.

Overall, most of the research evidence of incredible changes supports around fifteen to twenty minutes of meditation practice twice a day—once in the morning and once in the afternoon or early evening. Most people tend to start with a shorter, perhaps ten-minute practice. Some styles are useful before bed to put you into a restful sleep, while others are not designed to practise before bed as they create a state of mental alertness. Instructions vary across different techniques. Most teachers would have you sitting in a comfortable position with your back straight, while others may instruct you to lie down. The only general rule seems to be that something is better than nothing. Once a day is better than none a day. Two a day is better than one a day, and the more consistent you are, the more cumulative benefits you will reap. From here, the choice is yours.

The four main types of meditation that have been disseminated in the Western world are focussed-attention, loving-kindness, open-monitoring, and transcendental meditation techniques. Many people start with focussed attention and loving-kindness meditation in the form of audio guidance, which is widely available on many apps. The focussed attention style is the one that most people consider to be the sport of meditation itself. Others encounter the open-monitoring (Vipassana) or transcendental meditation technique through a short course or retreat with an experienced teacher. Despite the different techniques, the intentions, mental positions, and results of meditation practices overlap. All forms of meditation, practised regularly, can help us develop insight: a clear awareness of exactly what is happening in the conscious awareness as it happens.

FOCUSSED ATTENTION

Let's start with the most well-known type of meditation: the focussed attention technique guided by a teacher. The meditations can vary greatly in length, general style, and intention. A common form of guided meditation is a body scan. The instructor guides you to mentally scan the sensations in your body from the end of your toes to the top of your head. The breath serves as a focal point, as you gently bring your attention to the sensations and feelings of your breath moving in and out of your body. When your mind starts to wander off, as it will, you simply notice and gently bring your attention back to the body. Some exercises involve making mental notes of the thoughts or emotions arising before redirecting the attention back. For example, when the mind starts thinking about the future, the noting may be 'worrying' or 'planning'.

LOVING-KINDNESS

Loving-kindness meditation practices help us to be present moment to moment with full acceptance of emotions and sensations without judgement of them being good or bad. This reduces our experiential avoidance of short-term discomfort and can help us to show up in our lives more. In the next chapter, I will break down the techniques that focus on loving-kindness and compassion based entirely on working with the power of compassion in parenting.

OPEN MONITORING

Open-monitoring styles of meditation emerged from the Eastern practice of Vipassana. Vipassana is the Pali word for 'special seeing'. In Zen Buddhism, Vipassana is known to result in personal liberation and transformation that creates insight 'into the true nature of reality'. When learning Vipassana in the traditional way, a new student would attend a ten-day silent retreat, which would lay the foundation for their practice. This meditation practice involves sitting upright with your back straight and following the breath independently without specific external guidance and allowing the mind to 'just be' to cultivate a sense of calm alertness. During Vipassana, you may gently guide the attention to the breath, observing the breath and the body. Open and expanded awareness involves self-observation and self-exploration, improving a sense of internal attunement to the body, mind, and emotions.

This is the introspective process that helps us develop insight and, as Eastern teachers would describe, is a path to creating a more secure relationship with the self and others, including our children.

TRANSCENDENTAL MEDITATION®

Transcendental Meditation is a mantra-based meditation, sometimes also referred to as Vedic Meditation. This technique differs from other styles of meditation as it involves repeating a mantra silently, which is thought to serve as a tool to self-transcend. The mantra is traditionally a Sanskrit word, assigned by a teacher. It is usually practised twenty minutes, ideally twice a day. The mantra is often referred to as a 'vehicle' to deregulate and release stress, fatigue, and exhaustion from the nervous system—a very useful tool for modern parents—mothers especially. After the practice, it brings a sense of calm alertness and rejuvenation, as if you have just had a deep and restful sleep.

The clinical application of the Eastern Transcendental Meditation technique in modern psychology has been largely recognised due to the unique effectiveness, as a myriad of studies have shown, in reducing symptoms of complex trauma and suicidal depression in vulnerable populations, such as war veterans and incarcerated individuals, reducing the risk of reoffending.[34] The reason that I favour Transcendental Meditation as my personal committed practice is that it is simple, consistently effective, and can be practised independently—without reliance on external guidance. Ironically, I recently fell out of my practice routine as I navigated the nausea of the first trimester of pregnancy. Like each time I recommit, I notice very clear and obvious reductions in anxiety, distractibility, and irritability. This coincided with simultaneous improvements in my clarity of thought, creativity, mood, patience, compassion, and general feelings of joy—a lifeline for my own motherhood journey.

PART III

Staying Free

CHAPTER 9

Compassion: Unlimited Internal Resources

A few years ago, a mother named Natalie came to see me. She was struggling with low self-esteem and depressive symptoms, and her mind was plagued by feelings of worthlessness. Aside from her children, she felt her life had little meaning. She was extremely self-critical, in her words: grumpy, fat, explosive, up and down, and a loser. In our sessions, we were completely present with each other. I could feel her pain and suffering, and she could feel my empathy and compassion. I'm sure most people can recall a time when they have been so present with another person's pain and suffering that it's both beautiful and healing on both sides. In these moments, it's like you can see straight through their eyes and into the goodness of who they inherently are. Sometimes you can feel their pain to the point where your eyes well up with tears too. This is not to transfer our emotions, but to open ourselves enough to sit with their intense emotions in an authentic way. This moment was a full embodiment of empathy.

I guided her to imagine that her best friend was in the room, describing herself. Her words were self-critical and harsh, just like Natalie's. I asked Natalie how she would feel hearing her best friend speak so negatively about herself. She said she would probably feel very sad and compassionate towards her. When I asked how she would respond to her, she said 'with tenderness'. And what would she say to you if she heard this? She suggested her friend would say something caring ('I'm sorry that you're feeling this way'), reassure her ('You are feeling down right now, but you are none of those things'), and offer empathy to remind her that she is not alone in her feelings ('I often feel like that too').

Through this exercise, Natalie softened. Then I asked her to try and guess what I may be experiencing and thinking when I sit with her suffering. Tears rolled down her face as she answers with a smirk, 'a fat loser'. We giggled together. She smiled and acknowledged that she was being unfairly hard on herself and could recall bullying herself for a long time. How could she address this without working with her own heart?

Once she moved through her resistance to releasing her self-hatred and criticism, she was able to hold herself with a compassionate touch—hand over heart—and for a few moments, it brought acknowledgement to her suffering. This was step one. We discussed how the use of touch also worked to activate the parasympathetic nervous system, reducing cortisol and adrenaline and releasing oxytocin—a resource she was willing to bring to her parenting. With some modelling and practice, she was able to practise noticing when she was suffering and could bring a sense of kindness by saying things to herself like: *this is really hard...these emotions are intense...you're doing the best you can right now...how can I support you more?* Although it felt unnatural at first, she was eventually able to put her hand over her heart and say, 'Natalie, I love you.' Over time, she started to feel more secure within herself, which changed the way she showed up for her children.

COMPASSION AS AN EXPERIENCE

Maternal instincts are a pure form of compassion. We have been raised to give it, to try to find infinite resources of compassion and to know it at all times. We are taught and expected to *give* compassion, but we are not taught how to *experience* it. This is why we are left depleted of our internal resources. This is why when someone tells you to connect to your child's emotions, you may feel triggered. You give everything you can and feel as though you are left with nothing for yourself. This is the cycle of all cycles for exhausted parents.

Loving-kindness and compassion for others is a learned and practised skill that can become an infinite resource when we practise meditation based on compassion. I want you to imagine that compassion means your *heart* and *brain* have a unified sense of coherence, which creates kindness, non-judgement, generosity, and even security within the self. Compassion is experienced when the heart, body, and mind are working together simultaneously. Scientists are able to measure this physiologically within the nervous system and neurologically within the brain. The results are fascinating.

The research director of the HeartMath Institute, Rollin McCraty, suggests that when we change the 'rhythm of the heart', it alters communication with the brain, which creates a new baseline state and shifts our emotional experience.[35] Interestingly, he reports that the heart sends the brain more messages than the other way around. This aligns with the body of findings that show that meditating on loving-kindness and compassion changes the state of the body and traits in the brain. For parents, it is important to create a sense of coherence between the heart and brain, so that we can parent from the heart and not just from the mind. Parenting from the heart means interacting with our child from a core place of compassion. Then, all behaviour management and behaviour shaping comes from a place grounded in connection.

When we experience empathy fatigue or feel like we just can't find the inner resources to be compassionate to our child, it's a reflection of burnout. There is nothing wrong with us. We might be experiencing a sense of disconnection between our heart and brain. We know this place as the default mode. We may be parenting from the mind in relative isolation from more compassionate parts of ourselves. All seeking of authority and control over children comes from this part of the mind, which ultimately leads to parent–child disconnection.

Mindfulness and compassion are often described by teachers as a bird with two wings: both inseparable aspects of being able to fly free. This is why the word mindfulness is synonymously referred to as *heartfulness,* which captures the essence of coherence between the mind and heart. The process involves cultivating a sense of self-compassion in everyday life, learning to meditate on compassion, and parenting with radical compassion. This helps us use our deep love with a force for good.

Psychologist and researcher, Kristin Neff, defines self-compassion simply as showing ourselves the same kindness and care we would to a good friend.[36] She breaks down the process of cultivating self-compassion into three key steps. First, to have compassion for others, we must notice their suffering. Second, compassion involves feeling moved by others' suffering, so our *heart* responds to their pain ('to suffer with'). And third, we feel a sense of care and warmth with a desire to help the suffering person in some way.

We can follow the very same steps to cultivate compassion for other people, including our children. First, we must notice our child's suffering. This often means recognising their subtle or internalised emotional experiences, not just their behaviour. Second, we must feel their suffering in our hearts, which embodies empathy for their experience. And finally, we feel and show a sense of care and warmth to the child as they are suffering, which supports their emotional development.

When we experience compassion for someone else, we feel a sense of kindness, acceptance, and understanding when they make a mistake or fail in some way. It involves a sense of shared humility—that assumes we will all experience pain and suffering because we are human. It transcends the perceived hierarchy of an adult's suffering being more valid than a child's suffering.

CREATING PSYCHOLOGICAL RESOURCES

I can recall the first time I participated in a loving-kindness/

compassion meditation. I experienced a very rapid shift from feeling stressed, irritable, and disconnected to a calm, nurtured, warm, and connected feeling. We ended the practice by imagining that the loving-kindness we had just cultivated—strengthening the mind and heart coherence—was permeating outwards to all living things. This was my first experience early in my mindfulness journey. I was a little taken back, as I felt genuinely connected to all living things. I became intrigued by the science. Was this feeling and experience due to increased oxytocin—the love hormone—in my body? Is this how people conceptualised energy and consciousness? Finally, could this be what mystical people described as pure love? I feel slightly amused as I write this, because at the time, I thought the scientists were tricking the spiritualists. Now, I wonder if the scientists are only just catching up with the spiritualists.

There are parenting moments that occur every single day that afford the opportunity to practise heartfulness. In the midst of everyday difficulties or more distressing and unexpected events, bringing a sense of care and compassion becomes even more important—both for you and for your child. Regardless of the parenting stage, the research is congruent in finding that parent mindfulness and compassion is associated with lower anxiety and behavioural avoidance. In short, being kinder to yourself can improve the quality of your life. A 2018 study found that out of 387 mothers experiencing postpartum depression, those who had low or moderate levels of self-compassion experienced more negative attitudes towards motherhood and more frequent negative thoughts and beliefs about others' judgements made about maternal responsibility.[37] Thus, the harsher they were towards themselves, the more harshly they perceived other people to judge them.

We often perceive that other people's opinions are the problems, but we are sometimes blind to how we play a pivotal role in this cycle. Sometimes, the judgement is real, and at other times, it is imagined through our illusion of negative self-talk, which worsens depressive symptoms. It makes sense that practising self-compassion—which involves an element of presence rather than over-identifying with judgements—can help to reduce our psychological symptoms.

Self-compassion is different than positive thinking. When Natalie was experiencing negative self-talk spirals, I did not suggest that she change her cognition from 'I am a bad mother' to 'I am a good mother'. This would reinforce identification with the thoughts, stories, and judgements. Instead, mindfulness helps us become less identified, caught up, and fused with these stories. It helps us come back to the body and the moment. In this way, self-compassion is one of the biggest gifts you can give to new mothers, since it will help change the tone of the way they relate to their pain and suffering. If they maintain the practice, it will create new neural pathways and even lead to long-term change as their children get older.

We know from the research that to help parents become less judgemental of their children, it is essential that they first learn to become less judgemental of themselves. When we judge ourselves, we judge others, and we perceive that they judge us. Children are then thought to fuel their engine with the same substance as ours by default, mimicking our self-talk—critical or kind. This is why, if we want to raise resilient children, the embodiment of self-compassion is an essential skill to learn. It is key in breaking and changing intergenerational cycles in a way that self-nourishes, reinforcing you to maintain a new sense of self-kindness.

Loving-kindness and compassion meditations are sometimes referred to as metta meditation. The word *metta*, which emerges from the Eastern Pali language, translates to compassion, goodwill, and the quality of loving-kindness. The process of this type of meditation usually starts with directing loving-kindness towards ourselves and then expanding the feeling of compassion outwardly to others. This can include people we love, those we have conflicts with, those who we feel neutral about, and ultimately, all beings and living things. It is a vessel to deactivate the default 'I' egoic thinking and allows access to internal resources of kindness with humility of our own personal pain and suffering. This enables us to relate to the silent suffering of others.

Researchers have reported on fascinating research revealing the internal neurobiological and physiological effects of meditating on loving-kindness. The same team led by Richardson, who conducted the study on Olympic meditators (during metta meditation) also reported on some interesting findings after individuals participated in a two-week meditation program on compassion and loving-kindness.[38] The sample of participants was presented with emotive images designed to provoke empathy while their brains were being scanned. The brain scans revealed increased activity in circuits related to attention, perspective-taking, and positive emotions. In an experiment where they had to decide how much money they would donate to victims who had been cheated by a 'crooked dictator', the group of meditators offered twice as much money compared to the control group, who were non-meditators. It is not surprising that studies also show that meditators who focus on loving-kindness and compassion during meditation tend to have better emotion regulation and *show* more empathy to others in distress than those who meditate on empathy for others itself.

Particular brain regions associated with empathy—the secondary somatosensory and insular cortices—showed greater activation in the loving-kindness group. This is likely because focussing on empathy is more likely to exhibit negative emotions and greater distress, often referred to as 'empathy fatigue', when we are enmeshed with and inundated by another person's emotions. Empathy is a finite resource—we can get tired, burned out, and cynical without necessary boundaries around it. It's something that people in caring professions often learn the hard way. However, meditating on loving-kindness can counteract this depletion and restore our stamina to hold empathy for others.

Having and showing empathy in a genuine way is essential for helping children at all ages to feel heard, seen, understood, and secure. The power of these practices can be life-changing for stretched parents. We all have the ability to be the person who we want to be and to access higher and kinder parts of ourselves with the right resources and tools. We can embrace such practices as a way to meet our own hierarchy of needs, which helps us become self-sufficient and ultimately free.

SETTING LIMITS WITH COMPASSION

According to child psychology, if we were to break down the two most important aspects of parenting, they would be emotional attunement and limit-setting. Emotional attunement is the ability to recognise another person's emotional state, with an element of sensitivity. Sensitivity to emotions, paired with age-appropriate limits with consistency, creates attachment security. It's a safe base from which children can explore the world. Parenting with self-compassion and compassion for others can support emotional attunement. We can use this coherence between the heart and mind to connect with the mind state and emotion of the child. We will discuss the dynamic basis of attachment security in the next chapter.

First, I want to introduce a new concept as to how we can use *ruthless compassion* to help us become more consistent, fair, and secure in the way we relate to the self and therefore set boundaries for our children.

I first read of the idea of ruthless compassion in Bögels & Restifo's *Mindful Parenting* textbook.[39] They refer to limits as a form of 'ruthless compassion—something we do out of love for our children, which may at times be difficult for them and us' that is grounded in both acceptance and compassion. I have started to really take to explaining loving limits in this way. Although it makes logical sense that children and adolescents need boundaries, it can be difficult to set limits and remain consistent. It's a double-edged sword, because the less consistent we are, the more the boundaries are blurred for children. We may go through phases of allowing or ignoring a behaviour, and then we suddenly explode. This is a recipe for disconnection, and it creates ruptures and insecurity for the child if left unaddressed.

Another reason why I like explaining boundaries in this way is that ruthless compassion helps us determine if our boundaries are appropriate and necessary. So often, parents have particular rules that they enforce, try to control, and repeat stress cycle after stress cycle to reinforce. Much of the time, we are over-policing, over-reacting, and creating more stress in situations. Then, we end up too exhausted to pay attention to the times when such boundaries are incredibly important and necessary. Without awareness, we can deplete our energy on things that, at the end of the day, are mostly unimportant. When ruthless compassion for our child is the intention behind behaviour shaping, we approach situations more naturally focussed on connection and well-being rather than control and power. Marcia Sirota defined ruthless compassion as a concept that brings together fierceness, both in the pursuit of the truth (ruthlessness) and in our interactions with others and loving-kindness (compassion) towards ourselves and others.[40] It's an excellent combination to guide children and adolescents, as well as to keep ourselves accountable as parents to see things as they actually are.

In parenting, ruthless compassion means doing what is necessary to relentlessly respond with loving-kindness when making decisions with a child. It does not mean saying yes to make them happy immediately, and it often involves saying no with empathy. As a child psychologist, I have many conversations with parents about setting limits around technology, especially with children who have signs of addiction and obsession. However, these parents are terrified and often avoid setting consistent boundaries. Why? Because there is a huge consequence when they enforce it. The consequences can involve screaming, name-calling, hitting, spitting, having things in their home smashed, and so on. The child is likely to become angry and explosive when their addiction is taken away from them.

The way that our nervous system and brain have been designed makes it natural for us to shy away from these conflicts with our children. And millions of parents do, hence the statistics of technology addiction in young people. Without support, parents often report feeling like monsters setting limits around technology with children. When we reframe the idea of setting limits and enforcing boundaries with consistency based on ruthless compassion, their mindset shifts. They start to comprehend that the most loving and compassionate thing they can do is be consistent. Every single time they are not consistent or clear, they are not embracing compassion for how much their child needs their limit to create security for their well-being. Children and adolescents need support and containment for their well-being.

Another common cyclical experience is often reflected when a child has anxiety. This is because anxiety is not usually a solo inmate. If you experience anxiety yourself or parent a child with anxiety, you know that it is also accompanied by some recursive behavioural patterns and quite often poor sleep patterns. When I first meet parents who bring their child in for therapy to address anxiety, they are usually seeking help with managing the child's behaviour as well. It can be very difficult to strike a balance between being attuned to the child's emotions while supporting their anxiety and not reinforcing their undesired behavioural patterns.

For example, let's assume that Natalie's daughter, Daisy, experiences anxiety (emotion). She struggles to sleep (symptom), refuses to sleep in her own bed, wakes her parents multiple times a night (behaviour) and is often tired the next day (symptom). Therefore, she regularly refuses to go to school (behaviour). What often happens is that without support, Natalie ends up becoming anxious about the child's anxiety and reinforces behaviours that worsen her symptoms in the long run. She doesn't realise it because it happens slowly over time. While she needed support with an anxiety-management plan, including increasing Daisy's coping mechanisms, she also learnt to approach her nighttime behaviour and school refusal with ruthless compassion. Each time Natalie and her partner engaged with a fuss in the middle of the night and allowed her to stay home because she was too anxious, they were removing opportunities for her to improve. Once they worked with the school to ensure supports were in place, they reminded themselves by asking: what's the most compassionate thing I can do as a parent? The answer is usually drive them to school.

It doesn't mean ignoring a child's emotions or internal experience—it's quite the opposite. Part of a school refusal plan would involve having the parents and adults understand why she is refusing to go to school. Why is she anxious at school? Psychologists may also refer to this as the function of her behaviour. There is always a function of our behaviour. There could be many reasons, and it's our job as compassionate adults to find out. Here are some of the many possible reasons as to why Daisy doesn't want to attend school, which may be as simple or complex as:

- She is getting bullied in some way at school.
- She is struggling socially and is playing alone at lunchtime.
- She is struggling with her learning.
- She perceives one of the above to be true even if it isn't.
- She would prefer to stay home because she escapes uncomfortable feelings.
- She spends her day at home on technology, which rewards her behaviour.
- She gets one-on-one attention when she is at home with mum or dad.
- She is struggling socially and with learning because her attendance is irregular.

In these cases, parents often ask if they should enrol the child in another school. Most of the time, it is not the necessary solution. It obviously depends on the situation. Often the least compassionate thing we can do is allow this cycle to continue without addressing it for ourselves and for the child. This is where integrating self-compassion practices and meditation can help parents build up their stamina and energy to take the needed action. This could involve seeking help from a psychologist, making an appointment with the well-being team at school, or self-reflecting on what their role in the situation may be. It can help them address the empathy fatigue that would often have them avoiding the situation and their child in general. It may mean bringing in a contained time of the day where they aim to purely observe, connect with, and respond to their child without any interruption. Their only intention is to see beyond the surface with compassion for their child's full experience in the moment.

Just as Natalie could *feel* my compassion for her in our session, the child will likely feel the parent's compassionate empathy for their experience. This is the basis of emotional attunement. As the parent starts to feel more secure and balanced within themselves and in their connection to their child, they feel more able to do what it takes, even if it means saying no from a place of loving-kindness. They can give themselves permission to set necessary boundaries that ruthless compassion would require of them, even if it is in the middle of the night or in the morning. As we practise parenting—even during conflict—with a sense of heart and mind coherence, we create a safer emotional and psychological base for our children.

CHAPTER 10

Attunement: Insightful Parenting Skills

Have you ever heard someone from a generation before you mention they are sceptical about emotion-focussed parenting approaches? It may sound something like this, 'My parents didn't talk about emotions, and I turned out alright, didn't I?' Understanding attachment theory and the importance of secure parent–child attachment has been largely influential in shifting the commentary around optimal parenting styles. Attachment theory assumes that our adult attachment style is largely shaped by the earliest childhood attachments we have to our primary caregivers, usually our parents.

Attachment theory emerges from the early mid-century work of John Bowlby and his colleague, Mary Ainsworth.

Early proposals hypothesised that the responsiveness of the parent during the first eighteen months to two years of life determines the quality of the parent–child bond and has long-lasting effects on the child's social, emotional, behavioural, and cognitive development.[41] As infants are neurobiologically programmed to seek an emotional connection with their parents, the way that we respond and attune to infants can support the development of attachment security.

The first and second years of a child's life are the most influential in attachment bonding, reducing intensity by around three years old as children are better able to cope with periods of separation from early attachment figures without distress. According to this theory, which stands on decades of research underlying the field of child psychology, our early attachment can predict our attachment behaviour in adulthood, which impacts the quality of our life for years to come. Infants who have a secure attachment are able to play and explore freely from the safe base of their primary caregiver's presence. This is usually, but not always, their mother. If a father, grandparent, or carer is the primary caregiver, they too can be the primary attachment figure. A securely attached baby may or may not become slightly distressed when they are separated from their parent. However, the main difference is observed in the reunion when the caregiver returns. A securely attached baby is more easily soothed in the presence of an attachment figure who provides them with emotional security. Because they feel secure and responded to, they don't need to develop defences to their unpleasant emotions, and they can better express all their emotions.

If you have a sinking feeling in your stomach because your child is older than three years old and you're scanning through memories, practise self-compassion and continue reading. I am going to invite you to hold a juxtaposition in your mind:

- Early attachment security is the most important aspect of early childhood.
- Early attachment is not a destiny and can be improved and repaired with improved consistency in a parent's responsiveness, regardless of our starting point.

In early childhood, there are three distinct insecure attachment styles characterised by emotional and behavioural differences: insecure-avoidant, insecure-ambivalent (resistant), and insecure-disorganised.

INSECURE-AVOIDANT

Infants who are avoidant may seem indifferent to a stranger or parent and act unphased by separation from the parent. When reunited, the infant may avoid any closeness or emotional intimacy. The avoidance is a protective defence mechanism, and as they get older, emotional distance and withdrawal tend to be a pattern that they adopt to cope with their emotions. When children are avoidant, they do not positively reinforce the parent's attempts at emotional intimacy. The parent often feels like they are failing when they do make attempts. This can result in feelings of rejection, and their own inner child or punitive parent schema may take over their attempts to emotionally reconnect. Interestingly, these children are just as physiologically distressed when separated from their primary caregiver as secure children (measured by their heart rate, etc.) but have learned to suppress their emotions in order to reduce the risk of rejection. In other words, these insecure children actually require more emotional attunement and attempts for emotional intimacy, but they are just better at hiding it. When the parent learns to better self-regulate their own default emotional reactions to feeling rejected—especially their own schema wounds and ego—they become more equipped to recognise that their child's rejection or avoidance from them is actually representing how desperately they innately desire non-judgemental and unconditional attempts for emotional closeness.

When a parent is able to recognise that avoidance and withdrawal is a form of communicating their need for attachment and connection, they can learn to respond instead of falling into the spiral of self-blame and shame.

By learning to respond and facilitate emotional connection, even in these moments, attachment behaviour can be improved. If we assumed that attachment was fully formed by age three, it affords us no opportunities to improve. That would mean that our work as parents in supporting a child emotionally is complete. That is obviously far from true. It is important that we understand that attachment can continuously improve as we better understand ourselves and our children.

INSECURE-AMBIVALENT

Infants and young children who have an insecure-ambivalent attachment may be overly clingy but do not feel secure to explore or play. They may feel distressed when their parent leaves and, upon reunion, switch between being clingy and angry. They can be difficult to soothe and may physically struggle when being held. This can leave the parent feeling at a loss for how to respond. The parent may react to the clinginess with affection on one day and then become inundated by their child's demandingness, adopting a more punitive approach the next day. From the child's perspective, they may become hypervigilant to the parent's emotional state and internalise their inconsistency, which can be detrimental to improving attachment security. Thus, when children have separation anxiety or anxious temperaments, it is very important that the parent has self-care practices that help them to rebalance as the child's emotional security relies heavily on the consistency of their responsiveness.

INSECURE-DISORGANISED

Finally, the disorganised pattern of insecure attachment is less common and more problematic. The style develops when parents consistently fail to respond to their child's emotional distress. Children who experience neglect, emotional abuse, or trauma may develop this attachment style. Infants who demonstrate disorganised attachment may be distressed when separated from their parents but remain distressed when they are reunited. There is a difficult combination of needing and fearing their parent. Instead of making genuine attempts to connect emotionally or helping the child to self-soothe, such parents may mock or laugh at their child's expression of emotions, yell at them to intimidate them to stop crying, or ignore them for long periods of time. These children are at risk of becoming dissociated from their emotions, thoughts, and memories as they grow older and feel a sense of detachment from their identity and the world.

Well-intended parents usually don't want to contribute to such patterns. They are unfortunately perpetuated by a parent's unresolved trauma, dysfunctional intergenerational schemas, and can be further complicated by mental illness or substance abuse. With the right therapeutic supports and professional family intervention in place, parents who recognise such unhealthy patterns can be part of the solution of cycle-breaking and can learn skills to help them become more emotionally skilful themselves.

SUPPORTING SECURE ATTACHMENTS

I know the topic of attachment can be overwhelming for conscientious parents because they rightfully want to raise securely attached children. However, how we view attachment is important. When we view it as a goal—something that we either achieve by a certain age or do not achieve—we try to control our child's emotional experiences, which reinforces the cycles of perfectionism. The thought of *my* child being insecurely attached can be incredibly overwhelming, which feels like evidence of failure as a parent. To facilitate secure attachments, we do not have to respond perfectly all the time. When parents become overly concerned with attachment parenting, instead of being responsive to the child's emotions, they can become preoccupied with trying to control their child's emotional experience. This is counterproductive to emotional intimacy and is a stress cycle within itself.

Instead of entering the present moment with open awareness, which is where true intimacy is cultivated, we can get caught up judging and intellectualising their behaviour, which often leads to self-blame. When it comes to understanding attachment behaviour, parents should view it as an ongoing *value*, rather than a goal to tick off and achieve. This creates space to embody compassion for the fact that we are human and not machines, and it also aligns with a value-oriented approach to parenting life. It makes space to understand that children are humans with different temperaments and personalities and can have other unique experiences that are upsetting them, from painful teething to allergies and everything else in between. When we view attachment as being dynamic, we create the internal resources to become more attuned to our child over time, which can improve the security of the safe base.

In order to foster secure attachments, we must have an understanding and awareness of our child's unique temperament. Most simply defined, temperament is the way a child responds to the world. It can be broken down into three categories: reactivity, self-regulation, and sociability. Just like parents, some children are more sensitive to being highly reactive and have more sensitive nervous systems that result in stronger reactions to change, trying new things, being in socially stimulating environments, and responding to triggering events. Their nervous systems have longer-lasting stress responses when activated. They tend to have more difficulty self-regulating and require more parental responsiveness, co-regulation support, and gentle encouragement. Other children have a more naturally regulated temperament and are more easygoing, able to self-soothe, and adaptable in social environments. The interplay of temperament and attachment security reflects the interplay of the nature and nurture of a child's emotional development.

All parents with more than one child can probably recognise the differences in the unique temperaments of each of their children. They may even recognise that they find one particular temperament easier to attune to. This is often naturally reflective of the child who has a temperament similar to theirs. The less naturally attuned a parent feels to one of their children, the more self-compassion they may need to have for that particular child. That's because it is often the child that we struggle to connect to the most who needs our sensitive attunement and responsiveness. Emotional maturity in parents is grounded in unconditional acceptance of who their child is. It helps to hold space for the child and adolescent to develop a sense of autonomy over time with the safety of the relationship as the base to which they can grow, develop, and explore in the world.

THE PARENT'S ROLE IN CO-REGULATION

When Mary came to see me, she felt deflated. Her child was happy in every environment that she wasn't. As soon as she was present, he instantly became upset and unsettled. She felt both rejected and angry. Upon exploring why this was so triggering for her, she had internalised that she had somehow failed with their bonding. She assumed he was insecurely attached, which sent her down reactive spirals, often ending in tears. She explained several examples of him pushing away from her, becoming unsettled around her, and struggling to soothe at her attempts.

I asked her what would make her feel like she was succeeding, and she said for him to be happy and settled around her all of the time. We reflected if this was a 'puppy goal'—a goal that only a very cute puppy could achieve. Our perfectionism is striving for our children to be like puppies: ongoing positive emotions, relentless loyalty that makes us feel good enough as carers, cheeky but only in a cute way, having a preference to be around us, giving us affection that makes us want to be around them, and of course, no longer crying when we pat and cuddle them. Setting goals to achieve an emotional experience for a child is setting us up for failure. This is a pattern that continues to emerge into later childhood and adolescence.

Mary asked what the solution was. The first thing we looked at was her expectations and rules: 'When I attune to his emotions, he should respond in a particular way.' We reframed her intention from controlling his experience to self-regulating so she could show up regardless of how he responds to her. Her new intention was to be able to self-regulate: to notice her heart racing, her breath constricting, and tension increasing in her body when he became distressed. She was to bring this awareness to her body and slow down her stress response by taking slow breaths, and to respond to herself with kindness. She may say something to herself in the moment like, 'This is really hard; you're doing your best' and then bring awareness to how many other mothers have struggled just like her, sending a well-wish to all mothers with young children, 'May you all be well.' This helps Mary shift from it being about her failure to a normal human experience, feeling less isolated and more connected in the moment.

Only when Mary better self-regulates can the parent–child duo better co-regulate. Co-regulation is the process where two individuals affect each other, and when one person regulates, they influence the other. Mary was initially waiting for her outcome to be achieved in order to be able to self-regulate. As you can see, we cannot hand over our power to an infant or child. Regardless of an infant, child, or adolescent's age, the parent has a responsibility to hold the space for the co-regulation process as the young person does not have the emotional maturity. As we improve attunement to our own emotions and triggers, we become better able to attune to our child.

EMPATHY IN PRACTICE

Once we can regulate our own emotional reactivity, we can learn to respond more skilfully to our children. Being emotionally attuned is an integral aspect of all healthy relationships. After years of clinical and research experience understanding parent–child interaction, emotional attunement has stood out to me as the most important parenting skill to be cultivated, practised, and improved. Infants are born with an innate need to be attuned to; their ability to thrive relies on their parent's responsiveness to their emotional cues. They require having their emotional state noticed and responded to in order to co-regulate, self-regulate, and thrive in their emotional development.

This need continues as they move through early childhood, which is why when Mary's intention became to simply respond to her son's emotions—without control of the outcome—their relationship naturally improved. She was succeeding because she was intentionally responding to him. She was showing up even when it was hard, and that became her measure of success. When we are attuned to children, we communicate verbally and nonverbally that we are present and that we see and understand them. They feel our presence, and that holds the space for them to express their emotions in a healthy way, even if they are distressed. By showing them that it is safe to express unpleasant emotions around and in front of you, and you respond with your body language (e.g., leaning towards, not away; offering touch), your words (i.e., 'I can see you're overwhelmed'), and your empathy, you are helping them to reduce their defence mechanisms by teaching them that it is safe to express their emotions around you. Their uncomfortable emotions are no longer something that we need to avoid but something that we welcome as opportunities to deepen the emotional connection.

After years of dismissing their child's emotions, I have seen parents with adolescent children learn to emotionally attune to them. This can create transformation in the relationship. Research actually shows that enhancing emotional attunement and protective attachment behaviours (with an emotion-focussed approach) is essential for creating secure environments around adolescents, especially if there is an element of risk-taking. There is a whole body of research that supports the idea that while early attachment is very important, it is not necessarily a life sentence. Early attachment is a way to understand why we have emotional reactions and particular defence mechanisms in interpersonal relationships that can often be maladaptive or unhelpful to the relationship in the long term.

As we develop into adulthood, we can play an active role in improving our own attachment behaviour too. Perhaps while reading the descriptions, you reflected on your own attachment patterns—those that show up in your relationships now and those that may have characterised your own childhood. Many of these create our unconscious schema patterns and perpetuate the intergenerational cycle of insecure parent–child attachments. However, we can always work to improve attachment behaviour in children, adolescents, and adults, regardless of our starting point.

Mindfulness increases our self-awareness of triggers and internal experiences to be able to recognise our own attachment patterns in relationships, to notice when we default to a schema mode, and to bring conscious awareness to the situation (i.e., the freedom of choice). Meditation creates a more secure relationship with ourselves. This plays a role in securing our attachment behaviour, rendering us less vulnerable to co-dependant and insecure behavioural patterns. If we can make these interpersonal improvements, it has the power to improve the relationship with our children or adolescent and be a positive and protective factor in their life. As a side effect, it will also likely ripple to our other interpersonal relationships—marital, co-parenting, friendships, extended family, with colleagues, and so on. Addressing these patterns in ourselves as adults and parents is the invisible inner work of developing 'social and emotional intelligence' in relationships.

To improve attachment security, we must embody consistency and responsiveness with two aspects of parenting:

emotional attunement (empathy) and clear boundaries (ruthless compassion). A practical step-by-step guide to *Emotion Coaching*, coined by world-renowned relationship expert, John Gottman,[42] outlines five essential skills that we can use to emotionally attune and set limits with children:

1. Being aware of your child's emotion.
2. Recognising your child's expression of emotion as an opportunity for intimacy and teaching.
3. Listening with empathy and validating your child's feelings.
4. Helping your child learn to label their emotions with words.
5. Setting limits when you are helping your child solve problems or deal with upsetting situations appropriately.

BRINGING EMPATHY TO PARENT-CHILD CONFLICT

Let's explore a practical example of a parenting experience of Kate, from earlier chapters, who has had a lifelong struggle with perfectionism and control. Through her courage to do her own inner healing, Kate set the intention to work on the strong reactions she had when triggered by her daughter. Kate had developed the self-awareness that her daughter triggered her and that she was struggling to relate to her daughter's temperament which was different from hers. She was also aware that her reactions were making her daughter more dysregulated, and they were contributing to further ruptures and disconnection in their relationship. She wanted to become more grounded and present in the face of her triggers and be able to pause and breathe before getting swept away by her intense emotions. Furthermore, she had developed self-awareness and emotional insight and had set the intention to improve her ability to accept and self-regulate her emotions using mindfulness skills.

One of the reasons she found self-regulation so difficult was because her daughter would scream things at her like, 'You're the worst mum ever; I wish you would die.' She was able to become aware of how this triggered her schema modes (vulnerable child and punitive parent), and just by recognising this, she was able to bring a sense of understanding to the intensity of the emotional experience (self-compassion). Kate's default reaction used to sound like, 'Well then, why don't you go and live with your grandparents? Maybe then you'll appreciate me. One day I will die, and you'll feel bad,' as well as some power-struggle personal attacks, such as, 'Why can't you just be easy for once? You're so ungrateful. I've been at work all day, and I come home to this bad attitude.' Kate, when in punitive parent mode, would scream and send her daughter off to her bedroom, which at times was necessary so they could both calm down.

A key reason why Kate needed to address this cycle was that her daughter was insecure and testing her mother's ability to hold emotional security for her. When Kate sent her to her room in a dysregulated state, it played a role in reinforcing her daughter's feelings of emotional insecurity and rejection, feelings and experiences that Kate recognised as a child herself—those that shaped her need for control and perfectionism. As her daughter did not *yet* have the skills or capacity to self-regulate, communicate her needs, or seek connection in a prosocial way that her mother deemed acceptable, it was Kate's responsibility to address this negative cycle.

Kate learned to cultivate nonreactive awareness to the words and practice, thereby training her own attentional bias to attend to her daughter's emotions, instead of just her hurtful words. Only then could Kate practise emotion coaching and slowly improve by moving through the five steps:

1. Kate started to notice her daughter's lower-level emotions as they would escalate throughout the day, rather than just the explosive emotional reactions. She was able to pick up on subtle cues from her facial expression and body language.
2. Rather than avoiding recognising negative emotions, she was able to move towards them. When her daughter did explode, she viewed it as an opportunity for

emotional intimacy and teaching rather than a personal rejection or a reflection of her as a parent.
3. Kate was able to hold a mindful listening space for her daughter more regularly. She would listen to her daughter's words, expressions, and tone of voice to validate how she was feeling—without reacting. Her intentions were to make her daughter feel *heard* and validated, not to be right.
4. Based on the cues she was picking up on, she would assist her daughter to label her emotions as low or high intensity, which would often assist her in regulating before erupting. For example, she would help her to recognise 'You seem worried...' or 'I can see that you're feeling angry...' The more she practised labelling her emotions, the more fluid and natural it became.
5. Kate felt more empowered to set loving limits gently, rather than demanding her daughter go to her room for long periods of time. Kate was able to articulate, 'It's safe to express your anger at home. I am here to help you, but it's not okay to say those words.' If they needed space to calm down, she learnt to articulate, 'It seems as though you need some cool-down time. I'm going to come back in ten minutes to see how you're feeling.'

Kate started to break intergenerational cycles in her family and shifted to an emotion-focussed parenting approach. Attunement is essential to know the mental and emotional experience of your child. They all have unique temperaments. The more we are attuned to their internal world, the more we can match our responses with their needs, especially when they show a different temperament and emotional style to us.

CHAPTER 11

Values: Your Own Navigation System

We spend a lot of time thinking about what *not* to do as parents, but what do we know about what we *should* do? And should we all take the same approach? I was speaking to a well-respected colleague about my plan to write a book. She asked what my book was about, and I simply said 'parenting'. She curled her lip, gave me a little nod of approval, and wished me luck. I felt her saying, 'Oh great, another parenting book,' which I could recognise because I have had an off feeling about parenting books for many years myself. Of course, there are some outstanding parenting books that I regularly recommend to parents. But as a psychologist, I often work with parents to *undo* some of the beliefs, attitudes, opinions, and rigidity they have picked up from books and blogs.

Let's assume that a mother named Melissa has read all of the books and has come to the conclusion that divorce is bad and that her children would be better off if she stayed in an unhappy marriage. When she deepened her self-reflection and clarified *her* core needs (to have intimacy, to be in a respectful partnership, to share quality time and experiences, to feel respected and loved, etc.) with her core values (connection, quality time, and respect), she made the decision to leave the marriage. Melissa was used to ignoring her own needs in order to provide for her children, but she was able to give herself permission to honour her needs. By aligning to her needs and values, she became a role model for her daughters. Through this process of gaining her own clarity, she realised that not all decisions were mere 'parenting decisions'. She had learnt to make decisions based on her personal needs and vitality as a sovereign being, knowing that her own well-being will impact how she shows up as a parent.

On the other hand, a mother named Rikki had fleeting thoughts about leaving her marriage. Between the routine tasks of having young children and being married, she felt trapped. She decided to leave the marriage as she felt unhappy and idealised the time off that she would have when the kids were at their father's. This gave her a sense of freedom that she deeply desired. When she leaned in a little deeper to clarify her core needs that were not being met (a sense of individuation and autonomy from her young family and the freedom to creatively express herself and to engage in physical activity) as well as her core values that she was not currently aligned with (freedom, creative expression, health, and well-being), she discovered she did not actually want to leave her marriage. She really loved and wanted to grow old with her husband. But she was looking for short-term solutions to escape in order to meet her needs.

Through this self-reflection, she was able to develop a discipline around set days of the week where she had free time out of the house to do as she pleased. This usually involved something that integrated her values and needs such as doing yoga, hiking while listening to something that inspired her, allowing herself to journal and write before bed, and so on. Once she got in the new habit of protecting this time with a sense of just how important it was out of self-respect—as if the sustainability of her family depended on it—she was able to integrate it more naturally.

Every day, many people Google things along the lines of 'should I leave my marriage?' and ask an algorithm to help them make an important life decision. Clarifying our core values gives us a sense of individuality and power. No one—not even a therapist—can tell us what our life and parenting path should look like. If both Rikki and Melissa looked externally for an expert to tell them what was better for their children, they might have taken a costly side-step to what was truly important to them. Yet they actually made seemingly opposite personal decisions. They both found an improved sense of meaning in life, in turn making them feel happier and more balanced as parents. By carving out time to be still, reflect, and ask themselves what their needs and values were, they also both discovered a sense of personal autonomy, which meant different things to each of them and their families.

When asked to define their values, people often describe themes, like 'parenting' or 'career'. But themes do not help guide our life path and direction. This is because they do not describe how we would behave on an ongoing basis as a parent or in a career. If we were a parent, what sort of parent do we want to be? If we had a career, what sort of person would we want to show up as in that career? Many people are parents, or have a career, without having alignment to their core values. For a mother especially, referring to a theme can be confusing and create internal conflict when making key decisions. Do I go back to work, or do I be a stay-at-home mum? Do I choose parenting or my career? Yet if we are already a parent, we have already chosen 'parenting' in one way or another. Thus, by becoming clearer on the qualities that we want to guide our behaviour on an ongoing basis, it's a more helpful guidepost to direct our life journey.

What's most important is if we are *embodying* our core values regardless of how we are spending our time. If we break down the themes of parenting and career, we may realise what we are actually seeking is connection and contribution at home and at work. So, if we are connected to our colleagues and feel a sense of contribution at work, but when we get home, we feel depleted and disconnected, we need to realign and detect barriers at home. On the other hand, if we feel a sense of connection and contribution to the home and within our family, we may experience a sense of 'balance' and vitality. If we attend work and feel distracted, not present, and that the work lacks meaningful contribution, our experience will likely shift. In this way, evaluating our core values is less about what we want to do and more the human being that we want to be on a daily basis.

When we adopt someone else's rules (e.g., 'I must be a stay-at-home mum to be good enough' or 'I must work so I have purpose'), it can result in life feeling unmeaningful. My favourite easy-to-digest definition of values was written by an amazing educator, Russ Harris. He described, 'values are our heart's deepest desires for the way we want to interact with the world, other people, and ourselves. They're what we want to stand for in life, how we want to behave, what sort of person we want to be, what sort of strengths and qualities we want to develop.'[43] From this perspective, regardless of the outcome or goal, success is found in how we behave.

Many parenting approaches promise a specific outcome,

such as to 'raise a resilient child', and they actually reinforce the idea that we can control their future. Which by now, you know is a reinforcer of the stress cycles making us less confident and present parents. In this case, the bad news is also the good news. There is nothing you can do to *guarantee* that your child's life will be free of pain and suffering. Instead of trying to control an outcome relating to our child (i.e., to have a resilient and optimistic child), values enable us to govern our own behaviour as a parent (i.e., to respond to my child with compassion, non-judgement, and empathy) regardless of what arises on the parenting journey. This approach to parenting is not only more effective but also holds us more accountable to our behaviour as a parent.

KEEPING OUR VALUES IN SIGHT
TABLE 1. LIST OF COMMON VALUES

Authenticity	Community	Freedom	Knowledge	Respect
Achievement	Competency	Fun	Leadership	Security
Adventure	Connection	Growth	Learning	Service
Authority	Contribution	Health	Love	Spirituality
Autonomy	Courage	Honesty	Loyalty	Stability
Balance	Creativity	Humour	Meaning	Success
Beauty	Curiosity	Influence	Openness	Status
Boldness	Determination	Integrity	Optimism	Trust
Compassion	Fairness	Justice	Peace	Well-being
Challenge	Faith	Kindness	Pleasure	Wisdom

The way we relate to our values will change at varying points in our lives. They are like a flexible guiding light, as opposed to a rigid rule. As we develop an awareness of our own values, we can develop self-awareness of our personal needs. As we look back on our life, there are often clues that these values were deeply important to us. Some hints may be things that you deeply care about, things that give your life a sense of meaning, and things that make you feel alive, radiant, and as if your life is worthwhile. On the other hand, you can also find hints by looking at things that make you feel less vital when life feels more mundane.

I was recently offered an opportunity where I would work in a way where they were happy to essentially overpay me. However, I would not be doing anything meaningful. I would have to trade a specific amount of time—even if I was given no work during that time—to be available. I very quickly turned this opportunity down, and the organiser questioned in a confused tone of voice, 'But we're happy to pay you for the whole day even if you just work for one hour.' I said no because it would move me away from several of my core values of trust, integrity, and autonomy. This is one small example of how our values can serve as an *internal reinforcer* to become more influential to us than external reinforcers, like money, power, and status.

In my experience, making decisions based upon my values is rarely the easier option in the short term. It's often the harder choice, but it's the one that follows our inner authority rather than external expectations. Writing this book is a good example. For a long time, it didn't make logical sense to make many other personal and professional sacrifices in order to write and publish this book with no guarantees. What makes it worth it for me is not dependant on the future success of the book, but rather on aligning with my core values that led me to take on this project in the first place. Had I not developed the self-awareness of my personal needs and values, or if I was still living in default mode, perhaps I would have accepted an opportunity that was not deeply meaningful to me instead of doing what was required to publish this book. Because I have developed a strong internal authority, I have been positively reinforced along the journey.

If as a parent, we value being kind and compassionate to our children, every time we lose control and scream at them, we are—usually unconsciously—making a choice to not act compassionately towards them. That's why we feel so guilty later, because our behaviour is not aligned with our valued intentions. The following day brings an opportunity to make a new choice. So often, our intention as parents is to teach our children to have good morals and values, but in the busyness of everyday life, we forget to model and embody them, which is the only real way to 'teach' children to have them.

For example, some parents choose to stretch all family resources to send their child to an expensive school, and then when the child doesn't get the results that are deemed acceptable, the parents put them down, put additional pressure on them, remind them how much it costs, and threaten to move schools. This manipulates children's emotions because they start to fear their sense of security, losing their friends, and having to build new relationships. In this example, the parents are using emotions to try to motivate them to do better. They say that it comes from their good intentions and best wishes for their child. The reason why they sent the child to this school in the first place was that they wanted the child to have academic success, and they wanted good values to be instilled in them. The irony is that they are not modelling them nor focussing on how they relate to their child each day with self-awareness. They are reacting based on goal-oriented outcomes, which are their own perception of the child's results and success. If they gained clarity that moral character is their core value, they would then start to develop accountability to behave in a way that models moral character.

Another very common example is when parents say they want more respect from their adolescents. Yet, they do not consistently show respect back. Perhaps they regularly make negative comments about what their child is wearing and how they appear, tell their friends embarrassing things about their child, mock them, and go through their diary and bedroom when they are at school. There is a lack of value-aligned congruence. If they valued respect *in the relationship*, they would be accountable to embody it. Lacking values in the parent–child relationship can come at a huge cost in the long run.

It is so easy to get caught up in our stress-response that is concerned with the imminent future. When we have lost our way, we can reconnect with our values as a parent. It can be helpful to try and tune into the foresight and hindsight of our future selves. We can do this by imagining that we are approaching the end of life. Imagine your answers to the following questions if we asked your eighty- or ninety-year-old self: What are you most proud of in your life? What brought you the most joy and sense of purpose? How do you feel about the way you behaved in your life? How do you feel about the way you behaved towards your children in the first and most influential five, ten, and fifteen years you experienced with them?

These questions make my heart beat faster. We must practise self-compassion if we are brave enough to ask hard questions and answer honestly. Then, imagine that your child is now an adult and is asked, at the end of your life, to describe you as a parent. What would you want them to say? What would they say about the way you acted towards them and the values you modelled and helped to instil in them? When we have an idea of these answers, we can start to detect themes in what are probably our core values in relation to the parent that we want to be here and now.

If you notice a gap between your desired future and life now, then we have highlighted an area for personal development. You have an abundance of opportunities to realign with what matters most to you. We spend a lot of time avoiding the discomfort of our own mortality. In a way, we are wasting an incredible opportunity to enrich our lives. When we act like our life is never going to end, it's easy to avoid making hard decisions, making hard changes, and doing hard things as if we will have time to fix it later.

Those who have near-death experiences consistently report that after their mystical experience of the other side of life, they have gained a deeper perspective of life. In turn, they have changed the way they live with more openness and purpose. We don't have to have a near-death experience to make small or huge personal shifts that will change the direction of our life. It can be as little as 'Today I am going to…' or it can be as big as a life-changing decision to quit or commit to a job, leave or stay in a marriage, or take responsibility for our self-care. It's going to look different for everyone. The reason why it is hard is that it goes against the habitual defences that are designed to keep us safe and small.

VALUES-ALIGNED BEHAVIOUR CHANGE

To bring values to life in the context of parenting, we are going to explore some examples that adopt an ACT-based approach to meaningful behaviour change. You can use the same template to guide your own self-reflection:

1. Problem: what is the behaviour that needs changing?
2. Costs: what are the short- and long-term costs of avoiding this change?
3. Acceptance: what unwanted private experiences do we need to make space for?
4. Values: what core values motivate me to make this change in my life?
5. Action: what behaviours would align with making a helpful change?
6. Example: what is an example of a value-aligned behaviour?

In the following four case studies, we will use these questions to demonstrate specific applications of meaningful behavioural changes. Values-aligned plans can help parents get back on track and move their life in the direction that they desire.

Case Study 1: Erin is not implementing technology limits or boundaries with her son, but she is aware that she needs to for his own well-being.

Costs: sending him unclear and inconsistent messages, lack of boundaries, behaviour worsens, sleep regresses, family dysfunction increases, and ongoing conflict before and after technology.

Acceptance: anxiety, fear of his unpredictable response, feelings of rejection, stories about being a bad mother, and feeling guilty and hopeless.

Values: consistency and compassion as a parent and emotional well-being.

Action: any instance that involves using a timer and sticking to the agreed daily time limit out of ruthless compassion for self and the child. This involves being consistent when setting limits, regardless of her child's reaction.

Example: every single day where she has been consistent with limit-setting to the agreed forty-five minutes of screen time (gaming, YouTube, iPad, etc.) per school day and one hour on the weekend. Practising compassion for her son when he struggles and self-compassion for herself when it's hard.

Case Study 2: Anna is feeling burnt out. Her self-care is nonexistent, and her son's behaviour is becoming increasingly challenging for her to manage.

Costs: regressing emotional, physical, and psychological health and well-being, loss of sleep, making her symptoms and immune system worse, and inconsistent parenting approach to her son as she lacks inner resources.

Acceptance: thoughts and stories arising about why her self-care should not be a priority, discomfort with taking time to do nothing, and stories that self-care practices (such as self-compassion, meditation, and exercise) don't work for her.

Values: connection, vitality, and well-being.

Action: committing to at least thirty minutes of self-care every day.

Example: any instance of spending thirty minutes of time on a self-care task that is purely for her well-being and/or pleasure. It may be meditating, deep breathing, yoga, prayer, reading a book, walking in nature, singing, painting, or swimming.

Case Study 3: Ally feels disconnected from her toddler. She has identified that a lot of their interactions are transactional and lacking connection. She wants to start playing with her more without distraction but finds it difficult to make the time when she has a never-ending to-do list.

Costs: missing opportunities for connection and closeness, not giving her child full attention, often distracted, unable to savour beautiful moments, and the child learning to get attention through negative behaviour.

Acceptance: thoughts and stories arising about everything else she should be doing and all the reasons why she doesn't have time, physical tightening of her chest, and feelings of stress, anxiety, and urgency.

Values: trust, connection, and leadership.

Action: a period of time taken out each day for unstructured play and interaction where she gives her full attention to her daughter with the intention to purely respond to her, or in any moment where she pauses to savour the facial expression of her daughter, observing her play, or the way she speaks.

Example: paying attention to her daughter as a priority which may involve making eye contact, smiling, observing, playing interactively, paying attention to her in the bath, at dinner time, exploring nature together, and so on.

Case Study 4: Olivia has returned to work after being at home with young children, and she is experiencing a lack of balance between work and home life and responsibilities.

Costs: resentment towards her work for demanding too

much of her, resentment towards her kids for care demands, and feeling like she is constantly out of balance and overly stretched with responsibilities.

Acceptance: thoughts and stories arising about why she should want to stay at home with her kids, feelings of guilt on the days when she is at work, and making space for difficult conversations that may involve asserting personal needs and limits in partnership with her boss or with colleagues.

Values: balance, autonomy, and contribution.

Action: setting work hours and sticking to agreed hours, being present when at work and being present when at home (meaning not checking emails outside of hours), setting a limit when work expectations encroach on life balance, and protecting family quality time together. This may also involve self-care to rebalance.

Example: leaving work on time, not responding to texts, calls, or emails that involve work outside of agreed office hours, learning to say no, communicating with the necessary person when a project demands more than she has agreed to, and scheduling a planned leave in advance for a family holiday. Self-care may involve going to the sauna, going for a swim alone, walking in nature, or doing a cleanse.

There are so many ways that our life can be enriched by

getting clarity on our values and what is most important to us to support us in making choices—from the way we start our day to life-changing decisions. If you were to ask new parents what sort of parent they desire to be, they would likely list the most divine and desired traits. If you ask them again three, five, and ten years later, they might just giggle at their own 'naïve' intentions. Unrealistic or not, the innocent intentions are the foundation of the values that they had when they first entered parenting. Getting back in touch with our values in the midst of the difficult periods—which are inevitable in life—can help us to come back to our good intentions.

CHAPTER 12

Vision: Liberation and Life Possibilities

Freedom does not mean that we become liberated from all pain and suffering in our lives. It actually means the opposite. As a sensitive person who has always been inclined to lean into the deeper questions about life, it is clear to me how such inquiry without wisdom can create a greater sense of suffering. You may have noticed some uncomfortable feelings arising when reading parts of this book, as you perhaps related to some case studies and could empathise with the emotion behind our everyday struggles in parenting. More importantly, I hope that at some stage you asked yourself: how could I live life with more presence and liberation?

Many long-term meditators describe their life as 'before

and after meditation'. Before I learnt to meditate, I felt painful emotions and I attached to stories from the past and about the future. As a result of my empathy, I suffered from empathy fatigue and emotional burnout—both in my work and in my life. After four to eight weeks of meditation practice, I recall learning to relate to my thoughts, stories, and rules about myself differently. There was a recognition that *I* was not those thoughts and feelings, and I was able to notice that there was a part of the mind that notices.

The observing mind is able to witness and hold space for the painful emotions and creative stories we add to reality. It is able to witness how our thoughts and emotions lead to our behaviour and actions with self-awareness without judgement. The observing mind is pure awareness of our internal private and external experiences in the present moment. It feels like a wise and expanded sense of self. You can call it whatever you like—your true, authentic, wise, or higher self. The language that we use to describe experiences of awareness is far less important than the awareness itself.

Language, while necessary for humans and life-enriching in many ways, is the tool that we use to create separation. This includes the way in which we disagree, fight, judge, compare, and divide. It is important to be able to sit with ourselves in a way that is beyond the level of language.

We can observe our thoughts but still have a sense of distance from them. Committing to practices that develop our inner authority is experiential in the way we relate to our pain, suffering, and symptoms. This experience trumps talking about our problems over and over again and gives us tools to integrate new awareness and insights into our everyday lives instead. In this way, internal liberation comes from being able to transcend the level of language with awareness as our tool.

It is natural to notice a resistance towards meditation or simply engaging in stillness practices. If you notice an uncomfortable feeling at the thought of closing your eyes and sitting with yourself for twenty minutes, it is a reflection of the way that you currently relate to your own suffering. It is something that, after many years, I still experience when I fall off track from a regular daily practice. It often feels like there are more important things to do, or there is no time. Yet on any day of the year, if you checked my screen time on my phone, you would see a reflection of someone who does have time to sit down in stillness for twenty minutes. After many years of practice developing self-awareness, it becomes easier to recognise my own patterns of avoidance. I have cultivated the discipline to recommit to my ongoing practice. I have learnt to sit with my discomfort.

When I find myself back in the rhythm of daily transcendental meditation and insight practice, I instantly feel more like myself—my true self, not the constructed image I have of myself. This helps me relate to my own suffering and the suffering of others with more openness and compassion. Having practices to embrace the uncomfortable is the key to being able to gain a greater level of insight—in our own lives and in the way we view the world. It gives us a chance not to become inundated by negative emotions and turning to numbing tendencies. Once we have broken out of our habitual way of being, we can bring our enhanced self-awareness and awareness of others and regulate our emotions effectively. In part, it is because our window of tolerance in the nervous system has expanded, and we can hold the space to regulate stress more effectively. This makes us less vulnerable to be hijacked by auto-responses like changes in stress hormones.

Mindfulness interventions first gained respect within the biopsychosocial model of healthcare when studies showed that they were very effective in reducing suffering in those experiencing chronic pain. Instead of resisting and reacting to pain, we can cultivate non-judgemental and curious attention to the sensation of pain. The intention behind our attention actually alters how intensely we experience pain, both physical and emotional. By bringing non-judgemental pure awareness with kind intentions to our pain, we experience less suffering.

A huge pain point of collective suffering in modern life is the experience of loneliness. In a literal sense, we are more connected than ever. Yet, we are spiritually aloof as a collective. One reason is the overreliance on language to define our identity. We describe ourselves with the groups we are a part of, the school we went to, the profession we have, the roles we play, the postcode we live in, the illusion of status and hierarchy: the ego of life.

The year I wrote this book was a year of intense emphasis on how separately humanity is operating. With a global pandemic, a racial injustice movement, and existential concerns about climate change, we have been shown that we cannot survive separate from one another. Our well-being requires a sense of connectedness. Many people have friends but still feel alone. Many people are married but feel alone intimately. Many people go to work and feel empty and purposeless. Many parents feel disconnected from their children. Many children feel disconnected from their parents.

As a psychologist who works with different generations across the lifespan—children, adolescents, their parents, and their grandparents—at times, it's one of my greatest joys to observe the evolution of how we relate to our individual and shared suffering. Young people are starting to seek sovereignty from roles and limiting definitions that former generations experienced. They increasingly want to live a life that matters. I think that they actually *need* their sense of entitlement that many adults ridicule. They seem to discuss the big problems that we have left them, from injustice and inequality to climate change. They are the same generation of young people who are plagued by the epidemic of anxiety and depression. Many are not part of organised religion, especially in the Western world. Regardless, these amazing children and adolescents desperately need wise counsel. They are desperate for guidance in self-awareness, self-regulation, connection, and compassion.

This is where mindfulness practices can help to transform generations to come. Mindfulness and meditation—regardless if you include prayer or not—can be used as a tool to help people experience a level of awareness that is beyond the construct of human language. Some people refer to their experience as transcendent from the material, which coincides with a feeling of interconnection with ourselves, with others, and with the natural world around us. When we suffer, we can bring awareness to our shared suffering in humanity. Only once we experience a shift in the way we relate to our suffering can we model this for the next generation.

CONNECTING TO OUR HIGHER SELVES

Spiritual awakening means dissolving the illusion that you

are separate from oneness. It means losing your concept of self as you know it. As the field of psychology evolves, the way that we define well-being is a changed relationship with the way we relate to self. Long-term meditation practice leads to a neural change that reduces self-referential thinking. This may be experienced as moments of ego dissolution—a seeming loss of self-identity—during meditation. When practised over time, it translates to fewer thoughts about the self, interpreting events as relating to the self, and more pure awareness of what is. As we start to relate to and experience our self-identity in a different way, we are less fixated on the ruminative stories of who we are. Instead, we are present to who we are. This is what creates the conscious space to be able to pivot towards what's important and to participate in our own personal transformation.

As someone who has gravitated towards spiritual inquiry, I gain immense personal satisfaction and pleasure from understanding the psychological, scientific, and spiritual foundations of meditation. However, you do not have to be even the slightest bit interested in the intellectual aspect of this understanding in order to experience the mental health or life-enriching benefits. The change in the conceptualised and perceived self-image is important to give us the *freedom* to change as individuals and as parents.

Study after study shows that meditators experience an

almost unbelievable amount of side effects. It sometimes seems too good to be true. How could a daily practice of stillness have such a profound effect on someone's life? In the early stages of academic research in this area, many sceptics were understandably emphasising reasons to discount the optimistic research findings. Weak methodological studies, poor research designs, and countertransference of the researcher's motives, with many of the researchers critiqued for being biased meditators themselves. The latter is an interesting criticism because it would seem very ironic for a neuroscientist to understand the benefits of meditation and choose not to meditate themselves. However, over the last few decades, as research investment has proliferated and research designs have become more robust, sceptics will have a hard time resisting the science. The studies now speak for themselves. Anyone who wants to enrich their life should consider learning a meditation practice that works for them.

In daily life, when we wake up in the morning and engage in a morning meditation practice, it trains our attention to orient towards the present, moment by moment. This is where we find our flow states and the parts of the brain that have been activated in meditation. It helps us to have a sense of clarity of thought throughout the day. Because we are less distracted by our own stories, we also have a clearer sense of instinct and intuition.

Intuition is the ability to feel an inner sense of knowing without applying logical or analytical reasoning. Most people can relate to a time when they had a gut feeling about a person, a situation, or a decision. Like when we get a feeling of distrusting someone the first time we meet, or when we walk into a room and something just doesn't feel right. Or when we have an intuitive feeling to make a decision or take action on something that cannot be fully explained in a rational way. However, with hindsight, it often starts to make more sense. Intuition is thought to bridge the gap between the conscious and unconscious parts of our mind. The conscious mind is more thoughtful and logical, whereas the unconscious mind scans through files in our brain from the past, present, and future, connecting feelings in a nonlinear way, without our conscious awareness.

When it comes to parenting, there seems to be collective respect for a mother's intuition. From an evolutionary perspective, just like all other animals, humans too had to rely solely on intuition to survive and thrive. There were no parenting books, go-to experts, or information to read online. They had to rely heavily on maternal instincts. As we have evolved into a more sophisticated species, with an abundance of evidence and information to draw on, many of us have been taught to value external information over our instincts. In many ways, we are addicted to external validation.

When parents engage in regular meditation, they tend to develop more self-trust, which, I think, is related to more clarity of thought and enhanced intuition. Even in clinical practice, it presents again and again. Sometimes parents bring their child to see a psychologist as they just had a feeling that it was the right time to seek some additional support. And for whatever reason, it was. There are countless stories of parents who have a child with autism who had sought professional support from several different practitioners, who reported that nothing was wrong and that they would grow out of the behaviours of concern. Yet they persisted because of their gut feeling. Had they ignored their maternal intuition, their child may not have had access to the earliest intervention possible, which is well-documented to lead to the best developmental outcomes.

Other parents may have a child presenting with challenging behavioural traits, but they have a hunch that they have something else going on that requires medical attention first, like unaddressed food allergies, for example. They just follow their feeling that they need to seek an evaluation from a particular specialist. Cultivating freedom from needing validation does not mean rejecting external help. Freedom and liberation actually empower us to do the opposite by developing greater awareness of the help we need while maintaining a sense of sovereignty around our personal decisions.

In clinical practice, I often ask parents what their intuition says. Some look at me blankly or with a sense of frustration, and say, 'I don't know; that's why I'm asking you!' They have considered all the pros and cons in their mind a million times, but they remain in a state of paralysing fear (the freeze response). Others gasp a sigh of relief because they finally feel validated. When making an important parenting decision, there is always an element of uncertainty. What is the right answer? Do I move my child's school or stay? Do we move houses or stay? Do I work as a mother, or should I stay home? Do I stay in my safe job or take the risk? Do I make a life change, or do I continue pushing through? You can list all of the possible advantages and disadvantages of moving from their perspective, and still, there is no way to overanalyse the element of risk. No one can be sure.

Every time I read an email from a client who is *desperate* for a session to discuss a personal situation or decision that has arisen since the last session, I check myself in the mirror. How am I contributing to their dependence on external support? How can I help them to develop more stillness, connection to their intuition, and self-trust? Am I helping them to develop the tools they need to fish for life or am I giving them the fish? There are, of course, incredibly stressful and traumatic experiences where external support is essential, especially if we are living in unsupportive environments. I do not wish to minimise the role of therapy. However, I feel I am being conscientious and skilled at helping as a therapist when I am not actively reinforcing codependency in the client–therapist relationship in order to empower them.

Just like the parent–child relationship, we need to bring awareness to these patterns and try to empower one another even when it is not self-serving—especially when it is *not* self-serving. The practice of mindfulness and meditation helps us quiet the mind in order to hear more. We hear more by hearing less at the same time, more from our inner voice and less from the external world. If I can support my clients in learning to down-regulate their nervous systems and to develop skills to increase their internal resources, intuition, and values, then I feel that I am a skilled helper in breaking cycles.

HOLDING A VISION WITH PRESENCE

A juxtaposition of meditation is how it helps our mind to reduce time-travelling from the past and to the future. It helps us orient ourselves in the present, yet simultaneously helps us cultivate the mental space to hold a vision for the future. When meditation expands our awareness, and we can transcend our current life circumstances to gain greater insight, we develop a sense of metacognition. This is just like being able to gain heightened awareness and look down upon our life with a 10,000-foot view giving us the beauty of perspective. It is like a unique combination of calm acceptance of where we are now with a feeling of new possibility for the future. We use this insight to make conscious decisions about the future, which helps us become the active creator of our life rather than the victim of our circumstances.

The factors that have kept us stuck in the past, from our self-defeating habits to our perceived personality traits, become less important as we become more intentional moment to moment, day by day. This is the science of neuroplasticity and personal transformation. We learn to set new and conscious intentions based on our values. We deliberately try to align our behaviours that will help us move in the direction of our vision (of who we are and the vision for our lives) and engage in a daily meditation practice that deregulates the predetermined crevasses in our brain. It helps reinforce the new pathways that we are trying to practise and cultivate. It brings the foresight to ask ourselves: what is truly possible for my life?

Many people talk about the quest to have it all. Some people say that you can have it all, just not at the same time. I think meditation helps us question why we need to have it all. It helps us focus on having all that matters to us. We lose the need to be competitive with other people. What others seek to achieve becomes irrelevant to our balance and well-being. As we start to be driven by our internal reinforcements instead of the external world, the need for us to please others or maintain an external image of who we are starts to slowly dissipate. This is part of the freedom of self-sovereignty to make decisions, rather than reactions. We want to make conscious decisions that are aligned with our inner wisdom and the vision that we hold for our own life.

With this sense of meta-awareness and life perspective, it helps parents savour the moments that are truly important. It helps them shift from the tendency to police, control, try to change, and alter children in the name of building resilience. Instead, it focusses on being fully present, bringing acceptance, non-judgement, and compassion to their child and themselves. It gives them permission to make decisions based on a bird's-eye view of their values, ruthless compassion, and the emotional security of the relationship instead of responding from a default schema mode. It brings a permission slip to engage in the wonder of joy and allows us to create time to be together as a family without having to be doing anything.

The wonder of play itself brings a sense of connection. Children remember moments from their childhood. One of the most effective ways to teach children and to support children with developmental delays or disorders is to play with them. All attention to the person and reciprocal social skills—making eye contact, responding to the other person, turn-taking, cognitively comprehending the game, and developing receptive and expressive language—helps them be engaged and present in the act of playing. As they learn to pay attention, we are teaching them mindfulness.

Einstein defined wonder as a precondition for life. Mindfulness and meditation change parents and help them create space for wonder and joy in the whole family unit. Building families around presence, engagement, and play is *the* intervention for building a harmonious family life. We are active participators in bursting the illusion of finding happiness in the future, and we create a family culture of finding joy in the present.

Even during emotional or challenging experiences, we can create a culture around bringing curiosity to what we are experiencing. Then, without force, we notice what we have and feel like we have more, creating authentic experiences of gratitude. Just like joy, the experience of gratitude is found only in the present. If we want to raise resilient children, we have to create environments that help them to be present. To create environments for them to thrive in, we have to create environments so that we, too, can thrive.

We start to understand that relentless self-sacrifice is a recipe for disaster. Our needs are ultimately their needs. The more we live and thrive in the present, the more we can help them to live and thrive in the present. That results in more space for each of us to create and hold our own vision for the future. There are no other qualifications required. Although we still don't know everything about the human brain, there is one thing that I know for sure: meditating daily will change your life. Use it as a tool for your child to walk in your light and not in your shadow.

Acknowledgements

This body of work has been shaped by my life, academic, and clinical experiences. There are so many people whom I wish to thank, many whom I have been influenced by in person and many who have been influential to me through their work. To everyone who has been a part of this journey, I sincerely thank you.

I express gratitude to the thousands of people I have worked with individually, as a family, and in a group setting. I have gained just as much from you as you have gained from me. I feel it is both a privilege and sacred to hold a safe space for you when you feel most vulnerable.

I would not be here without the support of the psychology mentors who, at times, have gone above and beyond their duties to support my development as a psychologist. Special thanks to Jura Tender—you know how much I admire your life's work and support. Professor Dennis Moore—you believed in me and my work before mindfulness was respected. Janene Swalwell—for holding a safe supervision space for me to develop and reflect.

I would like to extend a special thanks to other psychology mentors, researchers, and educators whom I admire and who have helped me learn along the way—Professor Steve Hayes, Dr. Russ Harris, Dr. Shefali Tsabury, Professor Jon Kabat-Zinn, Professor Nirbhay Singh, Professor Susan Bögels, Dr. Esther de Bruin, Dr. Daniel Goleman, Professor Richard Davidson, Professor Daniel Siegel, and colleagues.

I would also like to express gratitude to other mentors who have had a profound influence on my personal and spiritual development over the years. Priscilla Darcy—for the most profound conversations that have helped me leap into this journey. Steve and Sue Griffith—for being such wise Vedic meditation teachers. Dr. Carolina Gonzales—for holding an important space for me at times when I needed it.

I extend thanks to everyone on my publishing team. The process of developing a manuscript to a published book involves a village of people behind the scenes. Thank you for your support and assistance. Natalie Aboudaoud—for being a supportive and organised publishing manager. Emma Rosenberg and Hal Clifford—for your editing and essential role in developing this manuscript. Rachael Brandenburg—for your creative input and cover design.

Most importantly, thank you to my dear friends and family. You know who you are and how much I appreciate you all. Special thanks to my mother, Kerrie, for raising me and providing the resources for me to complete such an extensive education. Parenting is the most important role we play in the world.

Finally, to my life partner, Jake. Words cannot thank you for your unconditional love and support. I could not have published this book without having you in my corner.

About the Author

DR RENEE CACHIA is an experienced Australian psychologist with a passion for empowering children, adolescents, and their parents to reach their full potential. As a published academic author with a Ph.D. in psychology and her own private practice, she is best known for her ability to uniquely integrate her research and clinical skills to help change and enrich lives with compassion.

Parenting Freedom is the book she has long dreamed of writing. Learn more at www.reneecachia.com.

Notes

1. Hayes, S. (2016). Psychological flexibility: How love turns pain into purpose. TEDx Talks. Retrieved from: https://www.youtube.com/watch?v=o79_gmO5ppg.

2. Goleman, D. (1995). *Emotional Intelligence: Why It Can Matter More Than IQ.* Bantam Books, Inc.

3. Siegel, D. J. (1999). *The Developing Mind: How Relationships and the Brain Interact to Shape Who We Are.* Guilford Press.

4. Robinson, P. J., Gould, D. A. & Strosahl, K. D. (2011). *Real Behavior Change in Primary Care.* New Harbinger.

5. Harris, R. (2007). *The Happiness Trap.* Exisle Publishing.

6. Gloster, A. T., Walder, N., Levin, M., Twohig, M. & Karekla, M. (2020). "The Empirical Status of Acceptance and Commitment Therapy: A review of meta-analyses." *Journal of Contextual Behavioral Science.*

7. Byrne, G., Ghráda, Á. N., O'Mahony, T. & Brennan, E. (in press). "A systematic review of the use of acceptance and commitment therapy in supporting parents." *Psychology and Psychotherapy: Theory, Research, and Practice.*

8. Tsabury, S. (2010). *The Conscious Parent: Transforming Ourselves, Empowering Our Children.* Namaste Publishing.

9. Miyagi, T., Oishi, N., Kobayashi, K., Ueno, T., Yoshimura, S., Murai, T. & Fujiwara, H. (2020). "Psychological resilience is correlated with dynamic changes in functional connectivity within the default mode network during a cognitive task." *Scientific Reports, 10,* 1–12.

10 Zhou, H. X., Chen, X., Shen, Y. Q., Li, L., Chen, N. X., Zhu, Z. C. & Yan, C. G. (2020). "Rumination and the default mode network: Meta-analysis of brain imaging studies and implications for depression." *Neuroimage, 206*, 116287.

11 Nolen-Hoeksema, S. (2000). "The role of rumination in depressive disorders and mixed anxiety/depressive symptoms." *Journal of Abnormal Psychology, 109*(3), 504.

12 Young, J. E; Klosko, J. S. & Weishaar, M. E (2003). *Schema Therapy: A Practitioner's Guide*. Guilford Press.

13 Singh, N. N., Lancioni, G. E., Medvedev, O. N., Hwang, Y. S. & Myers, R. E. (2020). "A Component Analysis of the Mindfulness-Based Positive Behavior Support (MBPBS) Program for Mindful Parenting by Mothers of Children with Autism Spectrum Disorder." *Mindfulness*, 1.

14 Bögels, S. & Restifo, K. (2013). *Mindful Parenting: A Guide For Mental Health Practitioners*. Springer Science & Business Media.

15 Kabat-Zinn, J. & Kabat-Zinn, M. (1997). *Everyday Blessings: The Inner World of Mindful Parenting*. Hachette Books.

16 Rusch, H. L., Rosario, M., Levison, L. M., Olivera, A., Livingston, W. S., Wu, T. & Gill, J. M. (2019). "The effect of mindfulness meditation on sleep quality: a systematic review and meta-analysis of randomized controlled trials." *Annals of the New York Academy of Sciences, 1445*(1), 5.

17 Gheibi, Z., Abbaspour, Z., Haghighyzadeh, M. H. & Javadifar, N. (2020). "Effects of a mindfulness-based childbirth and parenting program on maternal-fetal attachment: A randomized controlled trial among Iranian pregnant women." *Complementary Therapies in Clinical Practice, 41*, 101226.

18 Pickard, J. A., Townsend, M., Caputi, P. & Grenyer, B. F. (2017). "Observing the influence of mindfulness and attachment styles through mother and infant interaction: A longitudinal study." *Infant Mental Health Journal, 38*(3), 343–350.

19 4 Luberto, C. M., Shinday, N., Song, R., Philpotts, L. L., Park, E. R., Fricchione, G. L. & Yeh, G. Y. (2018). "A systematic review and meta-analysis of the effects of meditation on empathy, compassion, and prosocial behaviors." *Mindfulness, 9*(3), 708–724.

20 Lazar, S. W., Kerr, C. E., Wasserman, R. H., Gray, J. R., Greve, D. N., Treadway, M. T. & Rauch, S. L. (2005). "Meditation experience is associated with increased cortical thickness." *Neuroreport, 16*(17), 1893.

21 Bauer, C. C. C., Whitfield-Gabrieli, S., Díaz, J. L., Pasaye, E. H. & Barrios, F. A. (2019). "From state-to-trait meditation: Reconfiguration of central executive and default mode networks." *Eneuro, 6*(6).

22 Taren, A. A., Gianaros, P. J., Greco, C. M., Lindsay, E. K., Fairgrieve, A., Brown, K. W. & Bursley, J. K. (2015). "Mindfulness meditation training alters stress-related amygdala resting state functional connectivity: a randomized controlled trial." *Social Cognitive and Affective Neuroscience, 10*(12), 1758–1768.

23 Kaliman, P., Álvarez-López, M. J., Cosín-Tomás, M., Rosenkranz, M. A., Lutz, A. & Davidson, R. J. (2014). "Rapid changes in histone deacetylases and inflammatory gene expression in expert meditators." *Psychoneuroendocrinology, 40*, 96–107; Chaix, R., Alvarez-López, M. J., Fagny, M., Lemee, L., Regnault, B., Davidson, R. J. & Kaliman, P. (2017). "Epigenetic clock analysis in long-term meditators." *Psychoneuroendocrinology, 85*, 210–214.

24 Black, D. S. & Slavich, G. M. (2016). "Mindfulness meditation and the immune system: a systematic review of randomized controlled trials." *Annals of the New York Academy of Sciences, 1373*(1), 13.

25 Goleman, D. & Davidson, R. J. (2019). *Altered Traits: Science Reveals How Meditation Changes Your Mind, Brain and Body*. Avery Publishing Group; Lutz, A., Greischar, L. L., Rawlings, N. B., Ricard, M. & Davidson, R. J. (2004). "Long-term meditators self-induce high-amplitude gamma synchrony during mental practice." *Proceedings of the National Academy of Sciences, 101*(46), 16369–16373.

26 Lutz, A., Greischar, L. L., Rawlings, N. B., Ricard, M. & Davidson, R. J. (2004). "Long-term meditators self-induce high-amplitude gamma synchrony during mental practice." *Proceedings of the National Academy of Sciences, 101*(46), 16369–16373.

27 Adluru, N., Korponay, C. H., Norton, D. L., Goldman, R. I. & Davidson, R. J. (2020). "BrainAGE and regional volumetric analysis of a Buddhist monk: a longitudinal MRI case study." *Neurocase, 26*(2), 79–90.

28 Goleman, D. & Davidson, R. J. (2019). *Altered Traits: Science Reveals How Meditation Changes Your Mind, Brain and Body*. Avery Publishing Group; Adluru, N., Korponay, C. H., Norton, D. L., Goldman, R. I. & Davidson, R. J. (2020). "BrainAGE and regional volumetric analysis of a Buddhist monk: a longitudinal MRI case study." *Neurocase, 26*(2), 79–90.

29 Lee, D. J., Kulubya, E., Goldin, P., Goodarzi, A. & Girgis, F. (2018). "Review of the neural oscillations underlying meditation." *Frontiers in Neuroscience, 12*, 178.

30 Csíkszentmihályi, M. (2008). *Flow: The Psychology of Optimal Experience*. Harper Perennial Modern Classics; 1st Edition.

31 Csíkszentmihályi, M. (2008). Flow, The Secret to Happiness. Retrieved from: https://www.ted.com/talks/mihaly_csikszentmihalyi_flow_the_secret_to_happiness.

32 Zaccaro, A., Piarulli, A., Laurino, M., Garbella, E., Menicucci, D., Neri, B. & Gemignani, A. (2018). "How breath-control can change your life: a systematic review on psycho-physiological correlates of slow breathing." *Frontiers in Human Neuroscience, 12*, 353.

33 Pascoe, M. C., Thompson, D. R. & Ski, C. F. (2017). "Yoga, mindfulness-based stress reduction and stress-related physiological measures: A meta-analysis." *Psychoneuroendocrinology, 86*, 152–168.

34 Kang, S. S., Erbes, C. R., Lamberty, G. J., Thuras, P., Sponheim, S. R., Polusny, M. A. & Lim, K. O. (2018). "Transcendental meditation for veterans with post-traumatic stress disorder." *Psychological Trauma: Theory, Research, Practice, and Policy, 10*(6), 675; Nidich, S., O'Connor, T., Rutledge, T., Duncan, J., Compton, B., Seng, A. & Nidich, R. (2016). "Reduced trauma symptoms and perceived stress in male prison inmates through the Transcendental Meditation program: A randomised controlled trial." *The Permanente Journal, 20*(4).

35 Rollin McCraty. HeartMath Institute. Retrieved from: https://www.heartmath.org/science/.

36 Neff, K. Self-Compassion. Retrieved from https://self-compassion.org/.

37 Fonseca, A. & Canavarro, M. C. (2018). "Exploring the paths between dysfunctional attitudes towards motherhood and postpartum depressive symptoms: The moderating role of self-compassion." *Clinical Psychology & Psychotherapy, 25*(1), e96–e106.

38 Lutz, A., Brefczynski-Lewis, J., Johnstone, T. & Davidson, R. J. (2008). "Regulation of the neural circuitry of emotion by compassion meditation: effects of meditative expertise." *PloS one, 3*(3), e1897.

39 Bögels, S. & Restifo, K. (2013). *Mindful Parenting: A Guide for Mental Health Practitioners*. Springer Science & Business Media 269.

40 Sirota, M. Ruthless Compassion. Retrieved from: http://marciasirotamd.com/ruthless-compassion-institute.

41 Bowlby, J. (1979). "The Bowlby-Ainsworth attachment theory." *Behavioral and Brain Sciences, 2*(4), 637-638.

42 Gottman, J. The Gottman Institute. Emotion Coaching resources can be retrieved: https://www.gottman.com/.

43 Harris, R. (2009). *ACT Made Simple*. New Harbinger Publications, Inc.

www.ingramcontent.com/pod-product-compliance
Lightning Source LLC
Chambersburg PA
CBHW060520080526
44586CB00012B/549